MIXED MARTIAL

INSTRUCTION MANUAL / STRIKING

ANDERSON SILVA

WITH ERICH KRAUSS & GLEN CORDOZA

VICTORY BELT

CALIFORNIA

First Published in 2008 by Victory Belt Publishing.

ISBN 10: 0-9815044-1-8

ISBN 13: 978-0-9815044-1-4

This book is for educational purposes. The publisher and authors of this instructional book are not responsible in any manner whatsoever for any adverse effects arising directly or indirectly as a result of the information provided in this book. If not practiced safely and with caution, martial arts can be dangerous to you and to others. It is important to consult with a professional martial arts instructor before beginning training. It is also very important to consult with a physician prior to training due to the intense and strenuous nature of the techniques in this book.

Cover Design by Michael J. Morales, VIP GEAR

Printed in Hong Kong

CONTENTS

ATTACKS

COUNTERATTACKS

INTRODUCTION

As far back as I can remember, I adored the martial arts and idolized its practitioners. In my mind, Bruce Lee and Jackie Chan were nothing less than superheroes. I watched all of their movies several times over and dreamed of the day when I could learn the moves that allowed them to best any foe. But as a young child, my circumstances were less than favorable for realizing such a dream.

I had moved to Curitiba, Brazil, at the age of four to be raised by my aunt and uncle. They gave me warmth and values and taught me the importance of working hard in life, but with my uncle supporting a large family on a police officer's salary, martial arts classes were an unaffordable luxury. At least Curitiba was tranquil compared to Rio or São Paulo, and a child could always find a healthy way to entertain himself. So my days were spent playing soccer and video games with my friends.

Despite my days being filled with various sports and activities, I still found the time to hang around the local Tae Kwon Do academy where a couple of my friends trained. After class, I'd make a point to bother the instructor, Master Kangi, with all sorts of questions. I figured I might be able to pick up a few techniques here and there. As it turned out, my constant inquisitions paid off in an even better way. One day when I showed up, Master Kangi told me I could begin my training, even though I couldn't afford the tuition.

Rather unexpectedly, my life as a martial artist had begun. I trained every chance I could, and under Master Kangi's rigid discipline, I learned how to control my leg movements—an attribute that still saves me in fights today. The more I applied myself, the more my personality stabilized. I learned patience and the meaning of dedication. I wasn't an exceptional martial artist right out of the gate, but if I had trouble with a specific technique, I always adapted and found a way to make it work.

After many years of training, however, I still felt like an empty vessel. Master Kangi was a wonderful instructor and a great man, but I had a thirst to learn all of the martial arts. I didn't want to restrict myself to just one style. I began training in capoeira under Master Sergipe. I also trained hapkido. Anytime I learned a new technique, I considered it a wonderful and productive day. No matter how much knowledge was offered me, it was never enough.

I had a couple of close friends who trained Muay Thai, and sometimes they would practice at home, but they would never let me watch because I was still too young. Obviously, this only made my curiosity grow. It just so happened that I went to a school that was near Academia Kickbox, a Muay Thai school that was run by Master Edmar Cirilo Dos Angelos, and everyday on my walk home I would pass by his front doors. By chance, I had two other friends, Israel Gomes and Rodrigo Vidal, who happened to be students of Master Edmar. Just as I had with my friends at the Tae Kwon Do academy, I stopped by to talk with them every afternoon. Again I thought I could pick up a technique or two by watching, and again the instructor sensed my enthusiasm for the sport. I told him that I didn't have the money to pay for the tuition, but he invited me to come train nonetheless.

Muay Thai was quite different from Tae Kwon Do. While both arts strongly emphasize kicking techniques, Muay Thai also involves heavy training with punches; elbows; knees; and, most importantly, the clinch. Immediately I fell in love with the breadth of the discipline, how you could string the various techniques together to form complex combinations. Even when Master Edmar left the academy, I continued to train Muay Thai with my friend Rodrigo Videl, who took over as the instructor.

As with most who train in the martial arts, I eventually developed a hunger to test my skills. Muay Thai was quite popular in Brazil at the time, and there were frequent competitions. I partook in as many as I could. My instructors had stressed to all their students the importance of using technique rather than brute force, but for me this idea took on a special significance. Instead of embracing the brutality of the sport, I embraced the beauty of it. Of course, I enjoyed defeating my opponents, but how I earned a victory was just as important as the victory itself. My quest to embrace the "art" of fighting required me to attempt techniques other fighters might consider too risky, but the more I used those techniques in combat, the less risky they became.

My success with the striking arts was exciting, but I didn't want to stop there. I was already very intrigued with Brazilian jiu-jitsu, and I would have started at a much earlier age, but the monthly dues were even more expensive than Tae Kwon Do or Muay Thai. On top of that, you also had to purchase a pricey gi. Not willing to accept that the sport was exclusively for those who were better off, I began training at home with a couple of friends who had experience in the sport. We practiced without a gi, of course, but I got a decent introduction to the ground game.

The more time I spent grappling, the more I liked it. Eventually, I saved up some money, purchased a uniform, and began my official training with a number of different instructors. I started with Master Sonequinha, but when Elson Soneca opened a Gracie Academy in Curitiba, I spent some time under his wing. I also took some classes with Professor Roberto. But it wasn't until I fell under the tutelage of Professor Ramos that I began to make leaps and bounds. In addition to seeing me all the way up to purple belt, Professor Ramos introduced me to vale tudo.

I didn't wake up one morning and think, "Oh, I want to be a vale tudo fighter." It happened naturally due to my training. I wanted to test myself, just as I had in Tae Kwon Do and Muay Thai. By this time, I had trained in a number of different martial arts. Now I wanted to see how well I could put them all together in a competition where anything, other than biting and hair pulling, was legal. So I began entering small vale tudo events. In each of my fights, I tried to utilize techniques from all the various styles I had studied. I threw Tae Kwon Do kicks. I threw Muay Thai knees and elbows, and I used my knowledge of Brazilian jiu-jitsu on the ground. Successful not only in winning fights but also in fulfilling my goal of winning them artfully, I grew more and more interested in pursuing vale tudo.

My fights caught the attention of Rafael Cordeiro, the head coach at the world-famous Chute Boxe Academy in Curitiba. He invited me to come train, and I accepted his offer. Cordeiro was one of the best fighters around at the time, and as it turned out, he was also one of the best instructors when it came to vale tudo. I absorbed his knowledge like a sponge, as did all those under his guidance. For up to three hours a day, he versed me in an array of movements and positions on the ground. When training stand-up, he worked constantly on my elbow and knee strikes. He taught me how to be aggressive, and he forced me to hold on to my spirit and focus even when bone-tired. He taught me how to deal with pressure, to view my adversary with concentration, and to do my job swiftly and soundly. All of this was relatively easy to achieve because the entire academy was filled with like-minded individuals—individuals who were there to learn and fight. With time, we at Chute Boxe grew into a force to be reckoned with.

Training day in and day out at Chute Boxe, it was natural for me to want to put my skills into action. When Cordeiro thought I was ready, he entered me into Mecca 1, a vale tudo event that was partially being put on by Chute Boxe. This was in April 2000, I was twenty-five years old, and my opponent was Luiz Azeredo, a fellow member of Chute Boxe. Unfortunately, when I climbed into the ring, which was perched in the center of a smoky auditorium, I didn't bring the aggressiveness Cordeiro had taught me. After several rounds of action, the fight went to the judges' scorecards, and I lost the decision. Instead of letting the defeat get to me, I saw it as a positive experience. It was a good fight because it turned me into a man who respects all fighters, especially ones who had spent their entire life focusing on a single objective. After that night, I never underestimated an opponent again.

I took on Jose Barreto in the second Mecca event just a few months later. He was primarily a Brazilian jiu-jitsu practitioner, and realizing he wanted to take the fight to the ground, I did everything to keep the fight standing. When he tied up in the clinch in an attempt to snatch my legs and pull them out from underneath me, I established the Muay Thai clinch, positioned my elbows in front of his shoulders to keep him at bay, and threw knee strikes to his midsection and head. When he shot in from the outside to execute double-leg takedowns, I sprawled my legs back, dropped my body down on top of his, and then worked back to my feet while throwing strikes. In less than a minute, my strategy had worn him down, and he backed away to recover. This is when I employed the aggressiveness I had neglected in my first bout. I hunted him down, dazed him with several hard punches, and as he attempted to make his escape with his hands down, I landed a kick to his head that dropped him. The entire fight lasted a little more than a minute.

My next Mecca fight was four months later. With teammate Wanderlei Silva in my corner coaching me, I took on Claudionor Fontinelle, a competitor who had eight tough vale tudo fights under his belt. Although Fontinelle was built out of solid muscle, he was a good deal shorter than me. My game plan was to use my reach to my advantage and out-strike him, and that's just how things played out. Every time he threw a hard kick, I'd counter with a hard punch to the face. In one exchange a few seconds in, I countered with four or five hard punches to the face, causing him to duck low for a takedown. Thanks to all the work of my trainers, I was able to reverse his takedown and end up on top, allowing me to drive in more hard punches to his head. He managed to escape back to his feet, but keeping focused as Cordeiro had taught me, I quickly assaulted him with a flying knee to the face. Not pleased, he again tried to haul me to the mat. I countered with the Muay Thai clinch and more knees. A short while later, I even took him down and passed into side control. In the UFC you're not allowed to knee a downed opponent to the head, but this competition was in Brazil back in 2001, and pretty much anything was legal. So, I made use of the lack of rules and drove in some knees to his face from side control.

Fontinelle eventually escaped back to his feet, but at that point I knew he was no longer in the fight. His attacks were wilder and less frequent, allowing me to pick him apart with combinations. At around the six-minute mark, I backed him into the ropes and hit him with a combination that included two hard leg kicks, a cross, a knee to the face, and then another cross. When I landed the second cross, I put him down.

After Fontinelle, I fought one more time in Mecca. My opponent was Israel Albuquerque, and although the fight wasn't as action packed as some of the previous ones, it had an interesting ending. I had mounted Albuquerque and was punishing him with strikes. In an attempt to escape, he rolled over to his belly and stood up. Instead of sliding off his back, I cinched in a body lock and rode on his back, driving punches and elbows into the sides and back of his head as he staggered around the ring. Eventually, he collapsed and tapped out.

I felt my career had gotten off to a good start, but I knew I was far from being a name in the sport. I wanted to take things to the next level, and by chance, I got just that opportunity. After defeating Fontinelle, I got an offer to compete in Shooto, a Japanese MMA organization. I knew if I lost the fight, they probably wouldn't invite me back, so I wanted to put on a good show. My opponent was Tetsuji Kata, a competitor who'd had fifteen fights and only two losses, one of them being to the Shooto champion Hayato Sakurai. The fight went up and down, both of us trading strikes and submission attempts, but in the third round I managed to secure a triangle lock on my opponent. Although I couldn't secure it tight enough to choke him out, I used the position to land repeated strikes to his head. I wasn't able to put him away, but I had done enough to earn a judges' decision at the end of the three rounds.

As a result of my victory, Shooto invited me back. However, they had no plans to pit me against one of their mid-level fighters. They had me going up against Hayato Sakurai, the reigning Shooto champion. At that point, he had defeated six Brazilians in a row, and the organization's management was quite certain he would defeat another. They were certain they were sending a lamb to the slaughter. As one can imagine, I thought different. I knew it would be an extremely difficult fight, but I also knew that I had what it took to come out on top.

In the first round, I landed a good number of strikes while we were on our feet, causing Sakurai to take me down. Although I spent a decent amount of time with him in my guard, I nullified his attacks and constantly struck him from the bottom position.

In the second round, we also spent a good portion of time on the mat, but this time I was on top in Sakurai's guard instead of the other way around. He did an excellent job at nullifying my attacks, but it did little to earn him points on the judges' scorecards. Not satisfied with the damage I was causing, I stood up halfway into the round. This is where I got busy. I ducked Sakurai's haymakers and landed hard punches to his face and hard kicks to his legs. When he rushed forward, I tied him up in the Muay Thai clinch to keep him at bay. Eventually, I nailed him with some hard shots that caused him to turn away from me. I took his back, established my hooks on his legs, and secured the rear mount. Despite taking nearly a dozen hard shots to his face and blood draining from a cut under his eye, Sakurai refused to give up. The referee eventually halted the action to wipe away the blood and straighten his nose.

When the action restarted, I still had the back position, and I used it to land more hard strikes and sink in a rear naked choke. I squeezed with all my might, and still Sakurai refused to give in. Putting his massive heart to use, he hung on to the end of the round.

I began the third round picking him apart with strikes, but then Sakurai summoned some strength from deep down inside and managed to take me down. He ended up in my guard, where we beat our fists about each other's heads. I attempted to reverse my position several times, but Sakurai's base was strong. However, unsatisfied with the minimal damage he was causing, Sakurai stood up and again attempted to take me down, but this time I reversed him, put him on his back, and then struck his legs with kicks from the standing position. Eventually, he found an opening to stand, and I concluded the final round picking him apart with strikes. It was a much harder fight than

MIXED MARTIAL ARTS INSTRUCTION MANUAL

I had anticipated, and Sakurai was one hell of a fighter. But in the end, I received the unanimous decision.

Up to that point, I had been just another fighter. Defeating Sakurai put me on the map in a big way. In addition to receiving the Shooto title belt, I also received offers from other fighting organizations. It was decided that I would make the transition to Pride, which was also a Japanese fighting organization, just on a much larger scale. Shortly after I signed the contract, I learned that I couldn't fight in Pride. Apparently, I had also signed a contract with the UFC. At the time, I didn't handle any of the affairs concerning my profession. I let my managers take care of everything. In this situation, they'd had me sign contracts from two separate fighting organizations. I had been watching the UFC since it first started, and it always had been my dream to compete in the Octagon, but I knew nothing about their offer or the contract I signed with them. The end result was that I couldn't fight in either—I had a wait an entire year before I could step foot into Pride.

When I finally made it there, I defeated Alex Stiebling and Alexander Otsuka. For my third fight, I took on Carlos Newton. In addition to being a former UFC champion, Newton had tremendous skills in Brazilian jiu-jitsu, more so than most of the competitors in Pride. It was a proving ground for me. Did I have what it took to compete against one of the best grapplers in the world?

Shortly into the fight, Newton ducked underneath one of my punches and scored the takedown. Next, he passed my guard into side control. After landing a couple of strikes, he worked around my body and climbed into the mount. While he was throwing punches, I managed to escape and pull him back into my guard. To prevent him from passing again, I cinched down a triangle body lock. Both of us worked our strikes, but without much happening, the referee stood us back up. I had survived on the ground with one of the best grapplers in the world, and now it was my turn. I hunted Newton down with punches, and then when he ducked low for a takedown, I leapt for-ward with a flying knee, struck him in the head, and put him down. It was a huge victory for me because I was able to employ all the years of hard work I had put into Brazilian jiu-jitsu.

My next fight in Pride didn't go as well. While fighting Daiju Takase, he secured side control. I managed to reverse him and place him on his back, but when I did so, he locked in a triangle choke. It was deep, and I had no other choice but to tap in submission. In addition to suffering my first lost since my premier MMA bout, I was also having trouble with Chute Boxe. I felt the essence of the academy was turning. What had once united us and given us strength was being put aside. The values that had lifted the academy to such heights were being forgotten. The growth, fame, glory, and money had changed many of the people around me. To top this off, there was no clarification with our contracts. It had been a great experience. I owed so much to Master Rafael Cordeiro, Master Edmar, and to all my partners at the time, including Pele, Wanderlei, Nelson, and Master Sergio Chunha. They were largely responsible for any success that I'd had, but the academy had lost its essence, it's base, and it's Muay Thai characteristics. Things always change, and you need to be able to adapt to those changes to survive. It was my time to leave.

As a result of my decision, my career suffered. Immediately after I left, I wrote Pride a letter explaining my decision and that I would still like to fight in their organization. After all, fighting is my life. It's how I support my family. Unfortunately, they chose never to respond. Wanderlei was their superstar, and if they let me fight, they risked Chute Boxe pulling him from their roster. I got cast aside. It was a hard blow because I had never considered myself an athlete who simply competes in Pride, but rather a member of the Pride team. They ignored me for their own motives, and I was saddened by how it ended.

I continued to compete, but not on the scale that I had been. I took on Waldir dos Anjos in Brazil, Jeremy Horn in South Korea, and Lee Murray in England. I won each of these fights, but I was still struggling to get by. Pride ended up letting me back in for one event a year and a half after my loss to Daiju Takase, but again the cards weren't in my favor. I took on Ryo Chonan and dominated him all the way up to three minutes into the third round. Out of nowhere, Chonan jumped his legs into mine and executed a flying scissor heel hook. His timing and technique were perfect, leaving me with no choice but to tap out.

After that event, I went back to the smaller shows. I defeated Jorge Rivera and Curtis Stout in Cage Rage in England, and I got disqualified for knocking out Yushin Okami with an illegal kick to the face off my back at a Rumble on the Rock event in Hawaii. Next, I went back to Cage Rage and took on Tony Fryklund. That fight was a memorable one.

As I mentioned earlier, ever since I first started training I've hungered for new techniques. No longer fighting on the big stage, I had a lot of time between fights, and I'd read books and watch video tapes of traditional Muay Thai, or Muay Boran, in the hopes of picking up new techniques. Well, one day I was watching the movie *Ong Bac*, starring the Muay Boran phenom Tony Jaa, and I saw him defeat an assailant using a reverse back elbow. Immediately I thought, "that move looks like it would work." I tried to train it in the gym, but all my partners, including Videl, told me that there was no way it would work in a fight. Not wanting to give up on the move, I had my wife stand on the couch and hold out a pillow so I could do repetitions. She too thought I would get knocked out if I attempted it in the cage, but despite everyone's prejudice, I practiced the movement a hundred times, two times a week.

When it came time to step into the ring with Fryklund, I told my trainers that I was going to knock him out with it. Again they told me to forget the ridiculous reverse back elbow. That made me want to use it even more, so that's exactly what I did. Two minutes into the first round, I threw a reverse back elbow and knocked Fryklund out cold.

Despite being pleased with my performances, I considered giving up fighting. I needed to provide for my family, and that wasn't happening along my current path. I put my feelers out there one last time to see if I could drum up some interest with the bigger shows, and that's when the UFC offered me a contract to come fight for them. It was a huge opportunity and honor. I had been a fan of the UFC ever since it had begun, and I had dreamt about fighting in the Octagon, following in the footsteps of Royce Gracie, Don Frye, and Ken Shamrock.

Two months after my fight with Fryklund, I stepped into the Octagon for the first time and took on Chris Leben. To combat his aggressiveness, I utilized side-to-side movement, established dominant angles from which to attack, and then threw an assortment of strikes. I knocked him down with punches shortly into the first round; he got back up, and I knocked him down again with a knee to the face. The fight was over in under a minute, and I was back in the game.

I was sure that I would have to have several more fights before I got a shot at the title, but due to the quality of my techniques and my performance as a fighter, they gave me the opportunity right after I fought Leben.

I had deep respect for Rich Franklin, both as a person and as the middleweight champion of the UFC. I admired how he always remained so composed in the cage, and so I trained very hard for the fight. What allowed me to dominate that fight was the Muay Thai clinch. Where I trained in Curitiba, developing a strong Muay Thai clinch is a long tradition. All the professors have spent years mastering it, and they pass their skills on to their students. I had spent a good portion of my training on this position alone and even worked tirelessly on integrating new techniques with it to make it more applicable to MMA. I knew that every time a jiu-jitsu practitioner or wrestler goes for a takedown, he has to drop his head, so I learned how to defend takedowns using the clinch. It was one thing Rich Franklin didn't expect. When I tied up with him in the clinch, I felt considerably stronger. I used that strength to my advantage, and I got the victory and the title belt as a result.

After that fight, I had a number of good showings. I defeated Travis Lutter by catching him in a triangle choke and raining elbow strikes down on his head. I took out Nathan Marquart with strikes, and then I beat Rich Franklin a second time the same way I had beat him the first—using the Muay Thai clinch. With three title defenses under my belt, the UFC paired me up with Dan Henderson, a world-class wrestler and the former Pride middleweight champion. I was more anxious for this fight than any other. Henderson had defeated some of the top names in the sport, including a handful of Brazilians. I trained for that fight like never before. I practiced jiu-jitsu and takedown defense extensively with Antonio Rodrigo Nogueria and his brother Rogerio. I worked on developing my cardio around the clock.

My strategy was to let Henderson explode in the first round so that I could pull everything from him, make him exhausted. Then, in the second round, I would come out with explosive movements. In all of Henderson's previous fights, he had gone hit for hit. Every time his opponent hit him, Henderson would hit his opponent back. With Henderson packing a very powerful punch, it had worked out well for him. However, my strategy in the second round was to explode into him with a strike, and then explode back out before he could retaliate.

Luckily, my game plan worked flawlessly. In the first round, Henderson went crazy on the attack. Instead of fighting back, I weathered the storm. At the beginning of the second round, Henderson's tank was low and mine was full. I struck and moved just as planned, and it confused him. He tried harder and harder to get in that hit, and he burned more energy as a result. When he had no gas left whatsoever, I moved in for the kill and submitted him with a rear naked choke.

I had no plans on moving up a weight division, but one day I received a call from the UFC, asking if I could compete in the light heavyweight division. Immediately I called up my trainers in Brazil. "We have this fight at 205 pounds, but we only have forty-five days to prepare. What do you think?" We spoke for two hours, breaking down all that we could achieve in a training camp in that short of time. In the end, we decided that it was feasible and accepted the offer. If I hadn't felt like the UFC was now a part of my family, I probably wouldn't have accepted. But holding the title belt was a large responsibility, at least in my mind. I felt I had to help carry the UFC forward, even though they didn't need me for that task.

I put in the hard work, and when fight night came, I put on a show. My opponent was James Irvin, a formidable striker. In the opening round he threw a kick to the outside of my lead leg, and I used a technique you'll find in this book to catch his kick. Once I had it, I leaned forward, threw a cross, and knocked him out cold.

Being successful in two weight divisions in the most prestigious and competitive MMA organization in the world was a huge accomplishment for me. It made me realize that I had accomplished a large number of my objectives in fighting—but not all of them.

From here on out, I want to be a role model to new fighters. I must not only do my job in the cage, but also do it in a technical way that people find inspirational. I want to be remembered as a fighter who made a difference. I will continue to spend time with my family and do all the things that make me happy, such as playing soccer, paintball, and laughing for long hours with my friends, but I will also continue to test myself in the cage. Early in life I learned that what makes one great, the majority of the time, is discipline. If I can pass that on to others through constantly improving in each of my fights, my life and time in the sport will have been well spent.

1

STANCE AND FOOTWORK

STANCE

Before you learn footwork, punches, kicks, or takedowns, you must work on developing a proper fighting stance. It is very important that you do not rush through this portion of your training because your stance is your foundation. If your foundation is weak, everything you build on top of it will also be weak.

The first thing to be sorted out is which foot to put forward. Most choose to put their power side in the rear. For example, I'm left handed, so I tend to begin my fights with my left foot back and my right foot forward. This is known as a southpaw stance. However, during most fights I'll spend a good portion of the time with my left foot forward and my right foot back, which is called a standard stance. By switching back and forth between a southpaw stance and a standard stance, I'll often confuse my opponent.

Once you have chosen a natural stance and spent some time developing it, I strongly recommend learning how to fight with your opposite foot forward because it will open different attacking and counterattacking options. For example, when you and your opponent are standing in the same stance, meaning you both have the same foot forward, you have a different set of attacks and targets than you do when you

and your opponent are standing in opposite stances, meaning opposite feet forward. To demonstrate how your attacks and targets change according to the stance you and your opponent take, I've broken the attacking and counterattacking sections of this book into same stance and opposite stance techniques.

Once you've decided which foot feels most natural in the forward position, the next step is to work on the positioning of your body. Although this volume only covers striking, you want to develop a stance that allows you to employ all of the tools in your arsenal, which includes takedowns and takedown defenses. To help you achieve this, I demonstrate the high stance and the low stance in this section, but it helps not to think of them as two separate stances. In order to be an effective mixed martial artist, you must learn to transition between them fluidly.

Throughout the book I demonstrate striking combinations and counterattacks that require you to transition from a high stance to a low stance and vice versa. Many of these techniques also require you to remain mobile and throw strikes while transitioning from one stance to the next. If your transitions are awkward and you remain in a fixed position, your opponent will be able to read your movements and exploit holes in your positioning. The goal behind dropping and increasing your elevation while attacking and being under fire is to increase your offensive and defensive options, but this only works when you have mastered the stance change.

While it is important to play around with your stance to determine what feels most natural, there is one golden rule your stance must adhere to. For both the low and high stance, you must keep your feet staggered. If you assume a square stance, where your hips, feet, and shoulders are facing your opponent, you limit your striking options and make your body vulnerable to attack. By staggering your feet, you remain mobile. You can move forward, backward, and side to side with speed and explosiveness.

FOOTWORK

After mastering your stance, the next step is to tackle movement. In this section, I cover all the basic footwork that is required for both attacking and defending against attacks. The majority of the movements are not overly complex; the difficult part is not breaking your stance as you execute them. More specifically, you don't want to drop your hands, spread your feet too far apart, or do anything that will compromise your stance. The majority of techniques in this book require you to strike either while moving or shortly thereafter. If your stance falls apart the instant you employ footwork, these techniques will not be available to you.

To begin, start with the simple steps, such as side steps, forward and backward steps, and switching your stance. Once you get the hang of them, move on to pivot steps. The goal in this section is to get an introduction to the movements that you'll be using later in the book to set up attacks and counterattacks.

Instead of rushing through this section, take your time with it. Work on developing each technique, and then work on putting them together. Learning the side step may take just a few seconds, but it gets a little more complex when you combine it with a pivot. There are an infinite number of footwork combinations that you can put together, and the more you master, the more dangerous you become. While your stance is your foundation, your footwork is your ground floor. As long as your stance is sturdy and your footwork is balanced and fluid, you can build an assemblage of techniques that will allow you to weather any storm.

HIGH STANCE

The high stance is best suited for striking. Due to your upright posture, you can dish out punches, kicks, elbows, and knees without altering your elevation or foot positioning; this prevents you from telegraphing your movement and combinations. Assuming a high stance also allows you to efficiently block your opponent's strikes, including kicks to both your legs and head. In terms of mobility, your high center of gravity permits you to move fluidly from side to side and from front to back, all the while retaining your ability to strike and defend. In the photos below, I demonstrate how to assume a standard and southpaw high stance. It is important to pay special attention to posture, the placement of your feet, and hand and arm positioning.

Standard Fighting Stance

To assume a standard high stance, I place my left foot forward, stagger my feet slightly more than a shoulder's width apart, and distribute my weight equally on both of my legs. I point the toes of my left foot toward my opponent, and I point the toes of right foot toward my right side. My elbows are slightly bowed out to my sides, and my hands are up protecting my face. Notice how my left arm is extended a half of an arm's length away from my torso, and how my right arm is guarding the right side of my torso. To maintain my balance, I keep my knees bent and my back straight. From this position, I can strike as well as drop into a low stance, which would allow me to duck a punch or shoot in for a takedown.

Southpaw Fighting Stance

To assume a southpaw high stance, I place my right foot forward, stagger my feet slightly more than a shoulder's width apart, and distribute my weight equally on both of my legs. Notice how the toes of my right foot are pointed toward my opponent, and the toes of my left foot are pointed to my left. With my upper body, I bow my elbows slightly out to my sides and keep my hands up at chin level. Notice how my right arm is extended about a half an arm's length away from my body and my left arm is protecting the left half of my torso. To maintain my balance, I bend my knees slightly and keep my back straight. Once in position, I can strike as well as drop into a low stance, which would allow me duck underneath one of my opponent's strikes or shoot in for a takedown.

LOW STANCE

Although you'll most likely spend the majority of your time in a high stance while fighting, learning when and how to drop into a low stance has several benefits. First, it can be an excellent position to assume to counter your opponent's strikes. For example, when your opponent throws a punch or kick aimed at your head, you can avoid his attack altogether by dropping down into a low stance. Once his strike has sailed past, your opponent will most likely get thrust off balance from missing his target. This allows you to throw punches from your low stance or pop back up into a high stance and throw a more complex combination that includes kicks and knees. You also have the option of staying in your low stance and shooting in for a takedown, which is the second advantage. Due to your low center of gravity, you can explode forward, slip underneath your opponent's arms, and drive into his hips much more efficiently than you can when in a high stance. And when you execute a takedown immediately after ducking one of your opponent's strikes, your chances of being successful at hauling him to the mat increase significantly. Yet another benefit of learning how to drop from a high stance into a low stance is that you can often use the transition to fake out your opponent. For example, when you drop down into a low stance and step your lead foot forward, your opponent will most likely assume you are shooting in for a double-leg takedown and drop his guard to defend against your shot. The instant he lowers his guard, you have a clear opening to attack his head with strikes, either from your low stance or after quickly popping back up to a high stance. However, the low stance does have some restrictions. While it is an excellent position from which to throw punches, it isn't the best position from which to kick due to your low center of gravity. Along the same lines, it is also very difficult to check your opponent's kicks from a low stance. To be a versatile fighter and make use of all the weapons each stance offers, it is important not to think of the low stance and high stance as two separate positions. Instead, you should think of them as one position and become a master at maneuvering fluidly between the two.

Low Standard Fighting Stance

To transition from a standard high stance to a standard low stance, I bend my knees and drop my elevation. My weight is distributed equally on both of my legs, my back is straight, my left foot is pointing toward my opponent, and my right foot is pointed toward my right side at a forty-five-degree angle. Notice how my elbows are bowed slightly out to my sides, my hands are up protecting my face, my left arm is extended about half an arm's length away from my body, and my right arm is guarding the right side of my torso. It is also important to notice that I'm balanced on the ball of my rear foot. From this position, I can throw punches, explode forward for a takedown, or easily raise my elevation and attack from a high stance.

Low Southpaw Fighting Stance

To transition from a southpaw high stance into a southpaw low stance, I bend my knees and drop my elevation. My weight is distributed equally on both of my legs, my back is straight, my right foot is pointing toward my opponent, and my left foot is pointed toward my left side at a forty-five-degree angle. Notice how my elbows are bowed slightly out to my sides, my hands are up protecting my face, my right arm is extended about half an arm's length away from my body, and my left arm is guarding the left side of my torso. It is also important to notice that I'm balanced on the ball of my rear foot. From this position, I can throw punches, explode forward for a takedown, or easily raise my elevation and attack from a high stance.

SIDE STEP

Although employing footwork and movement is extremely important in a fight, you don't want to break your stance while doing so. To help prevent you from ending up in a compromising position that your opponent can capitalize upon, it's best to take small steps, leading with the foot closest to the direction you want to head. For example, if you want to step to your right, take a small step with your right foot and then slide your left foot into position. If you want to move toward your opponent, step forward with your lead foot and then slide your rear foot into position. No matter which direction you want to head, this rule applies. If you forget this rule and cross your feet, your balance will be compromised and your entire body will be vulnerable to attack.

In the sequence below, I demonstrate how to execute a side step. When employing this movement, it is important that you slide your trailing foot along the mat instead elevating it off the mat. This will help keep you balanced and poised for offensive and defensive movements. As you will discover later in the book, the side step can be done as an individual movement or it can be combined with other movements. For example, the side step can be the beginning of a sideways shuffle or you can immediately follow with a pivot to change your angle in relation to your opponent. The more footwork maneuvers you have in your arsenal, the easier it will be to create openings to attack, but first it is important to master the basics. The majority of attacks and counterattacks must be executed in the blink of an eye, and if you haven't trained the most basic footwork movements to the point that they've become instinctual, numerous opportunities will pass you by.

1 Lead Side Step (Standard Stance)

I've assumed a standard high stance.

2

I take a small outward step with my left foot.

3

I slide my right foot across the mat toward my left foot and reestablish my fighting stance.

1 Lead Side Step (Southpaw Stance)

I've assumed a southpaw high stance.

2

I take a small outward step with my right foot.

3

I slide my left foot across the mat toward my right foot and reestablish my fighting stance.

1 Rear Side Step (Standard Stance)

I've assumed a standard high stance.

2 I take a small outward step with my right foot.

3 I slide my left foot across the mat toward my right foot and reestablish my fighting stance.

1 Rear Side Step (Southpaw Stance)

I've assumed a southpaw high stance.

2 I take a small outward step with my left foot.

3 I slide my right foot across the mat toward my left foot and reestablish my fighting stance.

SWITCH STEP

To execute a forward switch step, all you have to do is step your rear foot forward. If you're in a standard fighting stance, step your right foot in front of your left. If you're in a southpaw stance, step your left foot in front of your right. Although it is an extremely simple technique, it can prove invaluable when hunting down a retreating opponent or while in the middle of a striking combination. By switching your stance, you create different angles of attack and force your opponent to adjust to your new positioning.

The backward switch step is the same as the forward switch step in that you reverse the positioning of your feet to assume an opposite fighting stance, but instead of stepping your rear foot forward, you step your lead foot back. This technique is best utilized when retreating after an attack or countering your opponent's forward movement. If you look at the photos below, you'll notice that as I step back I assume a low stance to position myself for strikes such as flying knees and punches. Assuming a low stance also better prepares you to defend against punches and takedowns.

Once you get comfortable with the forward and backward switch steps, practice sliding your lead foot backward and your rear foot forward at the same time, which allows you to switch your stance while remaining stationary. A good time to use this switch step is in the middle of a striking combination because it changes the side from which you can throw power shots. For example, switching from a standard stance into a southpaw stance allows you to throw powerful kicks and punches with your left leg and arm. As long as you don't telegraph the switch step by elevating your head or jumping, you can catch your opponent off guard with a powerful blow. With all three switch steps, it is important that you keep your feet spread a shoulder's width apart and maintain your balance at all times.

Forward Switch Step
(Standard to Southpaw)

I've assumed a standard fighting stance. To execute a forward switch step into a southpaw stance, I step my right foot in front of my left and turn my body in a counterclockwise direction.

Forward Switch Step
(Southpaw to Standard)

I've assumed a southpaw fighting stance. To execute a forward switch step into a standard stance, I step my left foot in front of my right and turn my body in a clockwise direction.

Backward Switch Step to Low Stance
(Standard to Southpaw)

I've assumed a standard fighting stance. Notice how my feet are spread roughly a shoulder's width apart.

I reverse the positioning of my feet by stepping my left foot behind my right foot.

I assume a low stance by rotating my body in a counterclockwise direction and distributing a larger portion of my weight onto my rear leg. From here, I'm poised to attack or defend.

Backward Switch Step to Low Stance
(Southpaw to Standard)

I've assumed a southpaw fighting stance. Notice how my feet are spread roughly a shoulder's width apart.

I reverse the positioning of my feet by stepping my right foot behind my left foot.

I assume a low stance by rotating my body in a clockwise direction and distributing a larger portion of my weight onto my rear leg. From here, I'm poised to attack or defend.

LEAD CROSS STEP

As a rule of thumb, you don't want to cross your feet when fighting because it jeopardizes your base and balance, but there are certain scenarios in which breaking this rule can work to your advantage. A good example is when both you and your opponent are fighting with the same foot forward. By cross stepping your lead foot to the outside of your opponent's lead foot, you change your angle. Suddenly you're no longer standing directly in front of him, but rather off to his side. Until he alters his stance, one whole side of his body will be exposed, creating an opening for you to attack. Boxers often utilize this footwork to slip a punch or attack their opponent's body, and wrestlers will use it to create an outside angle to shoot in for single-leg and high-crotch takedowns. However, in order to make this technique work for you instead of against you, there are two rules you must follow. The first is to never actually cross your lead foot in front of your rear foot. It's fine to line the heel of your lead foot up with the toes of your rear foot, but if you go any further, your base and balance will be nonexistent. The second rule is to immediately reestablish your fighting stance by sliding your rear foot into position. If you lag between executing the cross step and reacquiring your fighting stance, your opponent will be able to change his angle and knock you off balance by executing an attack of his own.

1 Lead Cross Step (Standard Stance)

I've assumed a standard stance.

2

Dropping my level slightly to maintain my balance, I step my left foot toward my right side. Notice how the heel of my left foot is lined up with my rear foot.

3

I reestablish my fighting stance by taking an outward step with my right foot.

1 Lead Cross Step (Southpaw Stance)

I've assumed a southpaw stance.

2

Dropping my level slightly to maintain my balance, I step my right foot toward my left side. Notice how the heel of my right foot is lined up with my rear foot.

3

I reestablish my fighting stance by taking an outward step with my left foot.

FORWARD STEP TO INSIDE PIVOT

Anytime you press forward into your opponent's comfort zone, you're going to generate a reaction. Most likely, he will either launch a counterattack or employ a countermovement. If he chooses the latter, his best course of action is to circle around the outside of your body. Not only does this take him out of harm's way, but it also changes the angle from which he can throw counterstrikes. In such a scenario, executing an inside pivot after stepping forward allows you to square your hips with your opponent's hips and eliminate his dominant angle of attack. The inside pivot can also work to your advantage when you step toward your opponent and he remains firmly planted on his feet. After stepping in with a couple of strikes, executing a quick pivot step changes your angle and makes one whole side of your opponent's body vulnerable. Before he can square his hips up with your hips to eliminate your dominant angle of attack, you've already landed several clean shots. In the sequence below I demonstrate how to execute the movements involved in the forward step to inside pivot, and later in the book I show how to use it to set up striking combinations and counter your opponent's attacks.

Forward Step to Inside Pivot (from Standard Stance)

I'm in a high standard stance.	Driving off the mat with my right foot, I step my left foot forward.	I pivot on my left foot in a clockwise direction. Notice how I maintain my stance as I execute this movement.	I continue to pivot on my left foot until I complete a forty-five-degree turn. Then I plant my right foot on the mat and reestablish my fighting stance.

Forward Step to Inside Pivot (from Southpaw Stance)

I'm in a southpaw stance.	Driving off the mat with my left foot, I step my right foot forward.	I pivot on my right foot in a counterclockwise direction. Notice how I maintain my stance as I execute this movement.	I continue to pivot on my right foot until I complete a forty-five-degree turn.

BACKWARD SWITCH STEP TO INSIDE PIVOT

Earlier in the section I demonstrated how to execute a backward switch step to reverse your stance, and now I take it one step further by showing how to execute a backward switch step to an inside pivot. As a rule of thumb, you don't want to retreat straight backward more than a couple of steps. There are of course a few exceptions to this rule, which I will cover later in the book, but for the most part retreating straight back gets you into trouble. Not only does it throw you off balance, but it also reduces your ability to defend against strikes or launch counterstrikes. When your opponent advances on your centerline, a better option is to step your lead foot back to reverse your stance and then execute an inside pivot. In addition to creating space between you and your opponent, it also changes the angle of your entire body. If employed at the right moment, the backward switch step to inside pivot will allow you to evade a potentially dangerous situation and make one whole side of your opponent's body vulnerable to attack. In order to avoid that attack, your opponent will have to square his hips with your hips, but in the time it takes him to accomplish that, you'll already have landed several clean blows.

Backward Switch Step to Inside Pivot (Standard Stance)

I've assumed a standard high stance.

I step my left foot behind my right to assume a southpaw stance.

I pivot on my right foot and rotate my body in a counterclockwise direction. Once I've completed a forty-five-degree turn, I plant my left foot on the mat and reestablish my fighting stance.

Backward Switch Step to Inside Pivot (Southpaw Stance)

I've assumed a southpaw high stance.

I step my right foot behind my left to assume a standard stance.

I pivot on my left foot and rotate my body in a clockwise direction. Once I've completed a forty-five-degree turn, I plant my right foot on the mat and reestablish my fighting stance.

SIDE STEP TO INSIDE PIVOT

The side step to inside pivot can prove useful in several scenarios. For example, if you're in a southpaw stance and your opponent circles toward the outside of your lead foot, executing a side step can keep your hips aligned with his and prevent him from obtaining a dominant angle of attack. If he changes directions and begins circling toward the inside of your lead leg, executing an inside pivot again allows you to keep your hips square with his hips. By utilizing this simple technique, you can keep your opponent in front of you with minimal movement. The side step to inside pivot can also be used as an attack. For example, you may advance on your opponent's centerline with a series of strikes, and then execute a side step to inside pivot to acquire a more dominant angle of attack. As with all the footwork techniques shown in this section, I recommend practicing the movements while shadow boxing and sparring as much as possible.

Side Step to Inside Pivot (Southpaw Stance)

1 I've assumed a southpaw high stance.

2 I take a small outward step with my right foot.

3 As I pivot on my right foot, I rotate my body in a counterclockwise direction and slide my left foot across the mat.

4 When I complete a forty-five-degree rotation, I plant my left foot on the mat and reestablish my fighting stance.

COUNTERMOVEMENTS

ANGLE OF ATTACK

The ultimate goal in fighting is to utilize footwork to acquire a dominant angle of attack. It's a simple concept—anytime you assume a position from which you can strike your opponent, and your opponent is out of position to hit you with a strike, you've acquired a dominant angle of attack. To achieve this positioning, you want your hips facing your opponent and your opponent's hips facing away from you. Not only does this allow you to throw strikes with less risk of getting hit with counterstrikes, but it also allows you to attack your target from odd, unpredictable angles.

The difficult part is not in theory, but in application. When you move, chances are your opponent will react to that movement to prevent you from acquiring a dominant angle. As a result, oftentimes the best way to achieve your goal is secure a dominant angle off of an attack or a counterattacking movement. In this section and the sections to come, I demonstrate many different strategies for establishing a dominant position. I suggest that you learn as many as possible. I also strongly advocate learning how to use footwork to reset your positioning when your opponent obtains a dominant angle of attack. In a bout between two evenly matched strikers, the one who is able to ac-

quire dominant angles of attack through footwork will always win the battle.

COUNTERMOVEMENT

Now that you have an understanding of basic footwork, I demonstrate how to use those movements to counter your opponent's attacks. I cover everything from slipping techniques to parries and blocks to checking techniques. In addition to demonstrating methods of evasion, I also demonstrate how to use evasive techniques to acquire a dominant angle of attack.

The reason I chose to focus on counters before attacks is because many of the attacks you'll learn later in the book involve countering movements. For example, to set up the lead power hook, you execute an outside slipping movement. As I have mentioned, the goal in any fight is to acquire a dominant angle of attack, and oftentimes the best way to achieve this is to utilize countering movements, even when you're not in danger of getting hit with a strike.

It is important to note that in this section I do not demonstrate how to follow up with an attack once you've evaded your opponent's strike and obtained a dominant angle using a countermovement. That will come later. Right now, it is important that you focus on honing your evasive skills through footwork.

EVASIVE TECHNIQUES

When your opponent attacks, it's best to evade his strike and counter with a strike of your own. For example, your opponent throws a jab, and you counter by slipping his jab and throwing a jab at the same time. If done correctly, just as your opponent's arm becomes fully extended, you crash your fist into his face. In addition to avoiding some pain and dishing some out, striking your opponent while he's in the middle of his attack breaks his rhythm, making it very difficult for him to follow up with more strikes. This allows you to go on the offensive.

Although I don't introduce counterstriking until later in the book, in this section you'll learn all the evasive maneuvers that are necessary for striking, such as slipping punches, leaning back to avoid punches, and sidestep counters. With each technique, be mindful of when and how you obtain a dominant angle of attack. It will help you down the road when you begin working on your counterattacks.

PARRIES AND BLOCKS

If your opponent is highly aggressive, sometimes catching him with a strike in the middle of his attack isn't enough to stop his assault. Other times, you might simply not have the right positioning to evade his attack. In either case, it is important to know how to parry or block his strike to avoid taking damage.

In this section, you will learn how to combine evasive maneuvers with parries and blocks to counter your opponent's straight punches, such as the jab and cross. You will also learn how to employ outside blocks and push blocks to counter your opponent's looping punches, such as the hook and overhand. Just remember, evading your opponent's strikes is always

best, but if you are unable to do so for whatever reason, blocking is your next best option.

CHECKING TECHNIQUES

In this section I demonstrate all the ways to block your opponent's kicks, including low kicks, mid-range kicks, and high kicks. The majority of techniques are rather simple. The hard part is developing the timing and reaction speed needed to be successful with the techniques. Although timing and speed can only come about through countless hours sparring and drilling, you can make this task a lot easier by spending time in the beginning to develop proper form. With all checking techniques, it is imperative that you keep your posture straight and your hands up for protection. To minimize the damage you take and increase the damage you cause your opponent, it is also important to angle your leg outward and catch kicks using the center portion of your shin. And lastly, stay relaxed and quickly pull your leg back into your stance. Retracting your leg before your opponent can pull his leg back into his stance allows you to launch a counterattack. Later in the book I'll give you a number of counterattacking options, but for right now it is important that you focus on the basics—form, timing, and speed.

EVASIVE TECHNIQUES

INSIDE SLIP

The inside slip is best utilized for evading straight punches such as the jab and cross. The movement involved is very similar to dropping into a low stance in that you lower your elevation by bending at the knees and sink your hips back, but instead of keeping your head centered, you move it away from your centerline by bending at the waist and tilting your upper body. Deciding when to use the inside slip can be a little tricky. If you have the same stance as your opponent, meaning the same foot forward, the inside slip can be used to evade his jab. If you have the opposite stance, the inside slip can be used to evade his cross. In both cases, it is important to keep your back straight and your hands up. This will protect you from other strikes in his combination and position you to launch counterattacks.

Inside Slip (Independent Movement)

I've assumed a southpaw high stance.

To execute the inside slip, I drop my level by bending at the knees and sinking my hips back. At the same time, I remove my head from my centerline by rotating my shoulders in a counterclockwise direction and dropping my head toward my left. Notice how I have kept my back straight and my left hand up to protect the left side of my face.

Inside Slip (Same Stance)

I've assumed a southpaw high stance and I'm squared off with Feijao in the pocket. Notice how we have the same foot forward. Due to this fact, I will be able to utilize an inside slip if he throws a right jab.

As Feijao extends his right arm, I sink my hips back, lower my elevation by bending at the knees, and dip my head toward my left side. Due to my actions, his punch sails past the side of my head.

Inside Slip (Opposite Stance)

I've assumed a southpaw high stance and I'm squared off with Feijao in the pocket. Notice how we are in opposite fighting stances. Due to this fact, I will be able to utilize an inside slip if he throws a right cross.

Feijao rotates his hips in a counterclockwise direction and begins to throw a right cross at my face. As he extends his arms, I begin rotating my shoulders in a counterclockwise direction and sinking my hips back.

As Feijao extends his right arm, I sink my hips back, lower my elevation by bending at the knees, and drop my head toward my left side. Due to my actions, his punch sails past the side of my head.

OUTSIDE SLIP

The outside slip is another movement that can be used to slip straight punches. Like the inside slip, the outside slip allows you evade a strike by moving your head away from your centerline. However, instead of repositioning your head by dropping your level, sinking your hips back, and bending your knees, you accomplish your goal by rotating your body and tilting your head in the direction of your lead leg. For example, if you have your right foot forward, you pivot on your left foot, rotate your hips and shoulders in a clockwise direction, and dip your head toward your right side (see Figure A). Once again, the stance that you and your opponent have will determine which strikes you can evade using the outside slip. For instance, if you and your opponent are in opposite stances (opposite feet forward), the outside slip can be used to evade his jab (see Figure C). If you are in the same stance (same feet forward), the outside slip can be used to evade his cross (see Figure B). No matter what strike you use the outside slip to evade, it is important that you keep your hands up at face level. This will help protect you from other strikes in your opponent's combination and allow you to launch counterstrikes.

(A) Outside Slip (Independent Movement)

1

2

I've assumed a southpaw stance.

Keeping my hands up to protect my face, I execute an outside slip by pivoting on my left foot, rotating my hips and shoulders in a clockwise direction, and tilting my head toward my right side. As I pivot on my left foot, notice how I keep my right foot pointing straight ahead to maintain my balance.

(B) Evading Left Cross with Outside Slip (Same Stance)

I've assumed a southpaw high stance, and I'm squared off with Feijao in the pocket. Notice that we both have the same foot forward. Due to our positioning, I can use an outside slip if he throws a left cross.

As Feijao throws a left cross toward my face, I begin executing an outside slip by pivoting on the ball of my left foot, rotating my hips and shoulders in a clockwise direction, and dipping my head toward my right side.

Continuing to rotate my body in a clockwise direction and dipping my head toward my right side, I successfully execute an outside slip and evade Feijao's cross.

(C) Evading Left Jab with Outside Slip (Opposite Stance)

I've assumed a southpaw high stance, and I'm squared off with Feijao in the pocket. Notice how we are in opposite fighting stances. Due to our positioning, I can use an outside slip if he throws a left jab.

As Feijao throws a left jab toward my face, I begin executing an outside slip by pivoting on the ball of my left foot, rotating my hips and shoulders in a clockwise direction, and dipping my head toward my right side.

Continuing to rotate my body in a clockwise direction and dipping my head toward my right side, I successfully execute an outside slip and evade Feijao's jab.

EVASIVE TECHNIQUES

DOUBLE SLIP

Now that I've covered both the inside slip and the outside slip, I demonstrate how to combine these movements to evade the common jab/cross combination. In the first sequence below, my opponent and I are in the same stance. As a result, I evade his jab utilizing an inside slip and then transition into an outside slip to evade his cross. In the second sequence, my opponent and I are in opposite stances, so I evade his jab with an outside slip and then transition into an inside slip to evade his cross. After drilling these movements thoroughly, switch things up by having your training partner lead with a cross and then follow up with a jab in both stance scenarios. Once you feel comfortable slipping straight punches, have your partner integrate looping punches into his combinations and evade them using the bob and weave, which is the next technique I demonstrate. The inside slip, outside slip, and bob and weave all work hand-in-hand with one another. The better you get at integrating these evasive maneuvers, the easier it will be to create openings to attack.

Inside to Outside Slip (Same Stance)

1

I've assumed a high stance and am squared off with Feijao in the pocket. Both of us are in a southpaw stance.

2

As Feijao throws a right jab, I dip my head toward my left and drop my level by bending at the knees and sinking my hips. Notice how the whole right side of his body is vulnerable to strikes.

Feijao follows his jab with a left cross. As his fist rockets toward me, I pivot on the ball of my left foot, rotate my hips and shoulders in a clockwise direction, and dip my head toward my right side. Notice how the whole left side of Feijao's body is vulnerable to strikes.

Outside to Inside Slip (Opposite Stance)

I've assumed a high stance and am squared off with Feijao in the pocket. I'm standing in a southpaw stance, and he is standing in a standard stance.

Feijao throws a left jab at my head. As his fist comes toward me, I pivot on the ball of my left foot, rotate my hips and shoulders in a clockwise direction, and dip my head toward my right side. Notice how I have dipped just far enough to avoid his punch.

As I move to reestablish my stance, Feijao rotates his body in a counterclockwise direction and begins to throw a right cross toward my head.

To slip Feijao's right cross, I dip my head toward my left and drop my level by bending slightly at the knees and sinking my hips back. Once again, notice how I have only dipped far enough to the side to avoid his strike.

BOB AND WEAVE

The bob and weave is best used to evade the lead and rear hook. To understand the movement involved, look no further than the name of the technique. The "bob" illustrates the up-and-down movement, while the "weave" describes the side-to-side movement. It's similar to the inside to outside slip in that you move your head from one side to the other, but instead of performing the majority of movements at the waist and remaining in a high stance, you drop down into a low stance and use your legs to produce the motion. Below I demonstrate how to evade a lead hook when you and your opponent are in opposite stances (opposite feet forward), as well as how to evade a rear hook when you and your opponent are in the same stance (same feet forward.) For the other possible scenarios, always bob and weave in the direction of your opponent's punching arm. For example, if you and your opponent are in a southpaw stance and he throws a right hook, weave your head toward his right side. Later in the book I demonstrate how to capitalize on the openings this evasive tactic can create.

Evade Rear Hook (Same Stance)	Bob and Weave (Independent Movement)	Evade Lead Hook (Opposite Stance)

I'm squared off with Feijao in the pocket. It is important to notice that in the left column both of us have the same foot forward, which allows me to evade a rear hook using a bob and weave. In the right column, we have opposite feet forward, which allows me to evade a lead hook using a bob and weave.

As Feijao throws a hook at my head, I drop my level by bending at the knees and sinking my hips back.

I slip Feijao's punch by dropping down into a low stance. Notice how I have kept both hands up to protect my face.

As Feijao's hook sails over my head, I begin weaving toward my right side by rotating my hips and shoulders in a clockwise direction.

As I weave toward my right side, I raise my elevation and assume a high stance.

OUTSIDE SLIP TO INSIDE PIVOT

Now that you understand how to slip your opponent's punches using head movement, I demonstrate how to combine that head movement with footwork to create dominant angles from which to attack. If you look at the sequence on the opposite page, you'll notice that I have my right foot forward and my opponent has his left foot forward. Due to our positioning, I evade his left jab using an outside slip and then create a dominant angle by employing an inside pivot. Notice how my movements have created an opportunity to attack the left side of his body. This exact technique could also have been used if my opponent and I had had the same foot forward, but instead of using the outside slip to evade his left jab, I would have used it to evade his left cross.

Outside Slip to Inside Pivot (Independent Movement)

1

I've assumed a southpaw high stance.

2

I step my right foot diagonally forward toward my right side. At the same time, I pivot on the ball of my left foot, turn my hips and shoulders in a clockwise direction, and lower my elevation by bending at the knees and dipping my head toward my right side.

3

I elevate my left hand and elbow to protect the left side of my face.

4

Placing a larger portion of my weight onto my right foot, I execute an inside pivot by turning my body in a counterclockwise direction and sliding my left foot across the mat.

5

Pivoting on my right foot, I continue to rotate my body in a counterclockwise direction. Once I've completed a forty-five-degree turn, I plant my left foot on the mat and reestablish my fighting stance.

Counter Left Jab with Outside Slip to Inside Pivot (Opposite Stance)

I've assumed a southpaw high stance, and I'm squared off with Fred. Notice how we have opposite feet forward.

Feijao throws a left jab at my face. As his punch comes toward me, I pivot on the ball of my left foot, rotate my hips and shoulders in a clockwise direction, and dip my head toward my right side.

As I slip Feijao's jab, I elevate my left arm to protect the left side of my face, step my right foot to the outside of his left foot to acquire a dominant angle of attack, and slide my left foot forward to maintain my stance.

Pivoting on my right foot, I rotate my body in a counterclockwise direction and slide my left foot across the mat.

I plant my left foot on the mat and reestablish my fighting stance. Having acquired a dominant angle of attack, I can now target Feijao's left side with a number of different attacks.

OUTSIDE SLIP / REAR CROSS STEP / OUTSIDE PIVOT

In the previous technique you evaded your opponent's strike using an outside slip, employed a side step to cover distance, and then utilized an inside pivot to acquire a dominant angle of attack. This technique begins the same in that you evade your opponent's punch using an outside slip, but to cover distance you employ a reverse cross step, and then acquire a dominant angle of attack utilizing an outside pivot. This technique allows you to close a lot of distance between you and your opponent upon slipping his punch, making it a good tool to have in your arsenal when up against a taller fighter with a superior reach advantage. In the sequences below, I demonstrate how to use this technique to slip a cross when you and your opponent are in the same stance (Figure A), as well as how to use it to slip a jab when you and your opponent are in opposite stances (Figure B).

Fighting Stance   **Outside Slip**   **Rear Cross Step**   **Outside Pivot**   **Fighting Stance**

1) I've assumed a southpaw high stance. 2) To execute an outside slip, I step my right foot diagonally forward toward my right side, pivot on the ball of my left foot, turn my hips and shoulders in a clockwise direction, and lower my elevation by bending my knees and dipping my head toward my right side. 3) Next, I employ a rear cross step by straightening my posture and stepping my left foot in front of my right. 4) To acquire a dominant angle of attack, I utilize an outside pivot by placing a larger portion of my weight onto my lead leg, pivoting on my left foot, and turning my body in a counterclockwise direction. 5) Once I've completed a forty-five-degree rotation, I plant my right foot on the mat and reestablish my fighting stance.

(A) Slip Left Cross (Same Stance)

I've assumed a southpaw high stance. Notice how Feijao and I both have our right foot forward.

Feijao throws a left cross at my face. As his punch comes toward me, I execute an outside slip by taking a small outward step with my right foot, rotating my body in a clockwise direction, and dipping my head toward my right side.

Having slipped Feijao's left cross, I close the distance between us by stepping my left foot in front of my right foot.

To acquire a dominant angle of attack, I employ an outward pivot by turning my body in a counterclockwise direction and pivoting on my left foot.

Having completed my pivot, I plant my right foot on the mat and reestablish my fighting stance. From here, I have several options for attacking Feijao's left side.

(B) Slip Left Jab (Opposite Stance)

I've assumed a southpaw high stance. Notice how Feijao and I have opposite feet forward.

Feijao throws a left jab at my face. As his punch comes toward me, I execute an outside slip by taking a small outward step with my right foot, rotating my body in a clockwise direction, and dipping my head toward my right side.

Having slipped Feijao's left jab, I close the distance between us by stepping my left foot in front of my right foot.

To acquire a dominant angle of attack, I employ an outward pivot by turning my body in a counterclockwise direction and pivoting on my left foot.

Having completed my pivot, I plant my right foot on the mat and reestablish my fighting stance. From here, I have several options for attacking Feijao's left side.

CROSS STEP TO OUTSIDE PIVOT TURN

In the footwork section, I introduced the lead cross step as a simple sidestep maneuver. Here I demonstrate how to use the lead cross step to slip your opponent's straight punches, and then follow up with an outside pivot to acquire a dominant angle from which to attack. When executing this maneuver, it is important that you step your lead foot across your opponent's centerline toward the outside of his body while dropping down into a low stance at the same time. If done correctly, the cross step and level change will move your head away from your centerline, forcing your opponent to miss with his strike. Once accomplished, employing the outside pivot turn will square your hips with the side of your opponent's body, allowing you to attack his vulnerable areas with a number of different strikes. If you look at the second group of photos, you'll notice that I'm standing in a southpaw stance and my opponent is standing in a standard stance. Due to our positioning, I use the lead cross step to outside pivot to combat his right cross. However, it is important to note that if my opponent and I both had the same foot forward, then I would use this maneuver to counter his right jab. This might seem rather complicated, but it's actually quite simple. If you have your right foot forward, then you'll utilize this technique to counter right-handed punches. If you have your left foot forward, you'll use this technique to counter left-handed punches.

Fighting Stance **Lead Cross Step** **Outside Pivot**

1) I've secured a southpaw stance. 2) To execute a lead cross step, I drop my level by slightly bending my knees and step my right foot toward my left side. 3) As my right foot touches down, I immediately step my left foot diagonally forward so that my feet are roughly on the same horizontal line. 4) Then, I execute an outside pivot by rotating my body in a clockwise direction and pivoting on my feet.

**Slip Right Cross
(Opposite Stance)**

I've assumed a southpaw high stance. Notice that Feijao and I have opposite feet forward.

Feijao throws a right cross at my face. To slip his punch, I utilize a lead cross step by dropping into a low stance and stepping my right foot forward and toward my left side. Notice how I've kept my back straight and my hands up to protect my face.

Due to my cross step, Feijao's punch sails past my head. Immediately I execute an outside pivot by rotating my body in a clockwise direction and pivoting on my right foot.

I continue to pivot on my right foot and rotate my body in a clockwise direction. Once I have completed a forty-five-degree rotation, I plant my left foot on the mat and reestablish my fighting stance. From here, I can attack Feijao's exposed right side.

LEAD PIVOT STEP TO INSIDE PIVOT

The lead pivot step to inside pivot is another effective countermovement that can be used to combat your opponent's straight punches. In the footwork section, I demonstrated how to execute a lead pivot step. I begin this sequence with that exact movement, but at the same time I also lean back and place a larger portion of my weight onto my lead leg. By combining the lead pivot step with the backward lean, I not only move my head away from my centerline, causing my opponent to miss his straight punch, but I also position myself to immediately follow up with an inside pivot. This last action allows me to square my hips with the side of my opponent's body and attack using my dominant angle. If my opponent were also in a southpaw stance, then I would have used this exact maneuver to counter his left cross.

(Opposite Stance)

I've assumed a southpaw high stance. Notice that Feijao and I have opposite feet forward.

Feijao throws a left jab at my face. To evade his punch, I execute a lead pivot step by taking a small outward step with my right foot, rotating my body in a counter-clockwise direction, and pivoting on my right foot.

3

Placing a larger portion of my weight onto my right leg, I lean back and continue to twist my body in a counter-clockwise direction. Due to my evasive actions, Feijao's jab sails by the side of my face.

4

I step my left foot backward.

5

To acquire a dominant angle of attack, I rotate my body in a clockwise direction. Notice how this squares my hips with the left side of Feijao's body. From here, I can attack his vulnerable left side with a number of different strikes.

OUTSIDE SLIP TO LEAD PIVOT STEP

In this sequence I demonstrate how to slip a punch by combining two evasion techniques—the outside slip and the lead pivot step. If you look at the photos in the right column below, you'll notice that I'm in a southpaw stance and my opponent is in a standard stance. Due to our positioning, the outside slip will be most effective for evading a left jab. However, if my opponent were also in a southpaw stance, then the outside slip would be most effective against a left cross. The best part about this technique is that it not only allows you to evade your opponent's strike, but it also gives you a dominant angle from which to attack. Later in the book I'll demonstrate how to utilize these movements in conjunction with striking combinations.

(Opposite Stance)

Feijao is in a standard stance and I'm in a southpaw stance. Both of us are looking for an opening to attack.

Feijao throws a left jab at my face. As his punch comes toward me, I utilize an outside pivot by rotating my hips and shoulders in a clockwise direction and dipping my head toward my right side.

3

Immediately after executing the outside pivot, I employ a lead pivot step by taking a small outward step with my right foot, placing a larger portion of my weight onto my right leg, leaning back, pivoting on the ball of my right foot, and rotating my hips and shoulders in a counter-clockwise direction. Due to my evasive tactics, Feijao's punch glides past the side of my head and I assume a perfect position to launch a counterattack.

4

I square my hips and shoulders with Feijao's left side and reestablish my fighting stance. From this dominant angle, I have many attacking options at my disposal.

THE REAR PARRY

The rear parry is a hand block that can be used to catch or redirect your opponent's straight punches. As far as movement is concerned, it is a fairly simple technique. The goal is to catch your opponent's fist in the palm of your hand as his arm reaches the end of its extension. The most difficult part is acquiring the proper sense of distance. Depending upon the distance between you and your opponent and the length of his arms, you can use the parry to either block his punch or use it in conjunction with a slip to evade his punch. For example, if your opponent is just inside of punching range and he throws a straight jab at your face, catching his fist in your palm is enough to prevent his fist from connecting with its target. If your reach is longer than your opponent's, you can also counter with a jab of your own at the same time (see sequence 1). As his fist lands in your palm, your fist collides with his face. Nice outcome. However, if your opponent is within punching range and he has a superior reach, catching his jab in your palm will not allow you to land a jab of your own. In such a scenario, your best bet for landing a counter jab is to slip your head away from your centerline and use the parry to guide his hand past the side of your face (see sequence 2). Although the parry is a simple technique to understand, the only way to develop the proper sense of distance is through countless hours drilling and sparring. I strongly suggest you invest that time because mastering this highly effective counter tactic is mandatory for becoming a proficient striker.

TECHNICAL NOTE

When using the rear parry you never want to reach your hand toward your opponent's punch. If you get into this bad habit, there is a chance your opponent will pick up on it. To break your guard, all he has to do is throw a fake punch. As your hand rockets forward, he pulls his hand back. Suddenly your face is exposed and vulnerable, allowing him to target it with other punches. To prevent such an outcome, move your hand in front of your face and let the punch come to it instead of the other way around. It is also important to note that in both sequences I'm blocking my opponent's right-handed strike using my left hand. If he had thrown a left-handed strike, I would have executed a lead parry with my right hand. As a rule of thumb, always parry with the opposite hand that your opponent is using to strike with.

Countering a Jab with Rear Parry and Counter Jab (Same Stance)

Feijao and I are both in a southpaw stance.

Feijao throws a right jab at my face, and I immediately counter by throwing a right jab at his face.

I move my left hand in front of my face and catch Feijao's fist in my palm. At the same time, I use my superior reach to my advantage by extending my right arm and landing a jab to his chin.

Countering a Jab with Rear Parry and Slip (Same Stance)

Feijao and I are both in a south-paw stance.

Feijao throws a right jab at my face. Immediately I dip my head toward my left side.

Keeping my head tilted toward my left side, I use my left hand to guide Feijao's right fist past my head.

LEAD HAND TRAP BLOCK

The lead hand trap is similar to the parry in that it allows you to redirect your opponent's straight punches. And just as with the parry, you execute the hand trap with your left arm when your opponent throws a right punch, and you execute the hand trap with your right arm when he throws a left punch. However, instead of catching his punch in the palm of your hand as you do when parrying, you use the outside of your lead forearm to redirect his punching arm toward the inside of your body. If your look at the photos in the sequence below, you'll notice that my opponent is standing in a standard stance and I'm standing in a southpaw stance. Due to our positioning, I use my right arm to intercept his left jab, and then I use this contact to force his arm downward and to the inside of my body. This allows me to avoid his punch, and it also creates many counterstriking options, which I cover later in the book.

Feijao is in a standard stance, and I'm in a southpaw stance. Both of us are looking for an opening to attack.	Feijao throws a left jab at my face. Immediately I extend my right arm slightly out and intercept the punch with the inside of my forearm.	As Feijao extends his arm, I redirect his strike away from my face by driving it downward and toward the inside of my body. Notice how this breaks his guard and creates an opening to attack.

OUTSIDE BLOCK

The outside block is best used to combat punches that approach from the outside, such as hooks and overhands. It's a relatively simple block in terms of movement, and when executed with the proper form and the correct timing, it can effectively protect your head from strikes. But due to the small gloves used in MMA competition, it can oftentimes be risky. It's not uncommon for a punch to slip through a crevasse in your protective shield and crash into the side of your face. And even when you utilize a perfect outside block, you're still absorbing the impact of the blow. A much better option is to slip or evade the strike altogether and position yourself to launch a counterattack. However, evading punches isn't always possible, especially when you're trading punches with your opponent. If slipping isn't an alternative, utilizing the outside block is certainly better than letting your opponent hit you. To lessen his chances of landing his blow, or at least minimize the impact of his strike, it's best to use the outside block in conjunction with strikes. Later in the book I demonstrate numerous counterattacks that you can employ off the outside block, but it is important to first learn the basic dynamics of this defensive maneuver.

Outside Block Independent Movement

I've assumed a southpaw fighting stance. To execute a rear outside block, I raise my left arm and reach my left hand behind my left ear. Notice how my left elbow is tight to my body and my right hand is positioned to launch a counterattack.

TECHNICAL NOTE

In the sequence below I utilize an outside block with my rear arm to protect myself from my opponent's right hook. If he were to throw a left hook or overhand, I could perform the exact same block using my lead arm.

**Defending Right Hook with Outside Block
(Same Stance)**

Feijao and I are squared off in the pocket. Both of us are in a southpaw stance.

Feijao throws a lead right hook toward the left side of my face. Immediately I rotate my hips and shoulders in a clockwise direction, elevate my left arm, and reach my left hand toward the back of my head.

Still rotating my hips and shoulders in a clockwise direction, I elevate my left elbow and reach my left hand behind my left ear. Having utilized proper timing and technique, I block Feijao's right hook and absorb the strike with my left forearm and shoulder.

LEAD ARM BLOCK

The lead arm block is used to counter straight punches such as jabs and crosses. It's different from the outside block in that it can be combined with footwork to create a dominant angle of attack and numerous openings to strike. To perform this block, the first step is to move your head to the outside of your opponent's striking arm. As his punch draws closer, the next step is to slide your lead forearm against the outside of his arm. With very little effort, you can then use your forearm to redirect his strike away from your body. Intercepting your opponent's punch in this fashion not only allows you to avoid a painful impact, but it can also mess with your opponent's rhythm and balance. Having forced his arm toward the inside of his body, there are usually numerous options for launching counterstrikes. Below I offer a couple of variations to this block. To learn how to use the lead arm block to kick-start an attack, flip to the counterattacks section.

**Counter Jab with Lead Arm Block
(Same Stance)**

Feijao and I are squared off in the pocket. Notice how we are both in a southpaw stance.

Feijao throws a straight jab at my face. Immediately I slip my head away from my centerline by rotating my hips and shoulders in a counterclockwise direction and dipping my head toward my left side. At the same time, I elevate my right arm and position it to the outside of Feijao's right fist.

As Feijao extends his right arm, I rotate my shoulders in a clockwise direction and redirect his arm to the outside of my body using my right forearm. Notice how my actions have positioned me to launch a counterattack.

Counter Cross with Lead Arm Block
(Opposite Stance)

I'm in a southpaw stance and Feijao has assumed a standard stance.

Feijao throws a right cross at my face. Immediately I slip my head away from my centerline by rotating hips and shoulders in a counterclockwise direction and dipping my head slightly toward my left side. At the same time, I elevate my right arm so that it makes contact with the outside of Feijao's right fist.

As Feijao extends his right arm, I rotate my shoulders in a clockwise direction and redirect his arm to the outside of my body using my right forearm. Notice how my actions have exposed his right side.

STOP BLOCK

The stop block is best utilized when in punching range to protect yourself from your opponent's rear hooks. The movement involved is similar to when you throw a straight punch, but instead of closing your fist and targeting your opponent's head, you keep your hand open and palm strike the shoulder of his punching arm. Generally speaking, straight punches are quicker than looping punches due to their straight trajectory. As long as you spot the hook early and are quick to react, your palm will reach your opponent's shoulder before his fist reaches your head. The instant you palm his shoulder, his body will get forced backward. This not only zaps the forward momentum of his punch, but it also knocks him off balance and makes him vulnerable to counterattacks. As with all countermovements, correct timing and proper form are imperative. If you fail to land your strike first or you palm the center of his body instead of his shoulder, you'll most likely take a nasty punch to the head.

**Counter Hook with Rear Stop Block
(Opposite Stance)**

I'm in a southpaw stance and Feijao is in a standard stance. Both of us are looking for an opening to attack.

Feijao throws a right hook at my head. Immediately I launch my counter by rotating my body in a clockwise direction, dipping my head toward my right side, and extending my left arm toward his right shoulder.

Before Feijao's fist reaches the side of my head, I drive my left palm into his right pectoral muscle, stealing all power from his punch. However, it is important to notice that I have elevated my left shoulder to protect the left side of my face. From here, I will follow up with a counterattack such as a right knee strike.

Counter Hook with Lead Stop Block
(Same Stance)

Feijao and I are both in a standard fighting stance.

Feijao throws a right hook at my head. Immediately I counter by rotating my body in a clockwise direction, dipping my head toward my right side, and driving my left hand into his right shoulder.

To zap all power from Feijao's punch, I drive my left hand into his shoulder and push him backward. Notice how I have elevated my left shoulder to protect the left side of my face. From here, I will follow up with a counterattack such as a right knee or right cross.

STANDARD CHECK

If you plan on entering MMA competition, it is imperative that you learn how to block your opponent's kicks. If you're nimble on your feet and have good reactions, it's certainly possible to evade or counter the majority of mid-level kicks by stepping out of the way, catching your opponent's leg, or landing a powerful strike before his leg crashes into your ribs, but there will always be that one kick you're not prepared to evade. It's also difficult to utilize these nonblocking options when your opponent throws low kicks because they have to travel less distance to reach their target. To prevent yourself from taking unnecessary abuse, I've demonstrated how to execute a lead and rear standard check in the sequences below. In addition to learning how to check kicks aimed at both your lead and rear legs, it is also important to spend an ample amount of time acquiring the proper timing. Unfortunately, this is not something that can be taught in a book. The only way to improve your timing is to drill both checks daily in the gym.

Lead Right Low Check Independent Movement (Southpaw Stance)

1

I've assumed a southpaw high stance.

2

Distributing my weight onto my left leg, I begin elevating my right leg straight up.

3

Staying balanced on my left leg, I elevate my right knee until it is at roughly the same height as my waist. Notice how my right leg is bent at a ninety degree angle, my hands are up protecting my face, and my posture is straight. These details keep me balanced and will allow me to quickly reestablish my fighting stance and launch a counterattack before my opponent can recover from his kick.

1

**Lead Left Low Check
Block Right Low Kick
(Same Stance)**

Feijao and I are both in a standard fighting stance, searching for an opening to attack.

Feijao distributes his weight onto his lead leg and begins rotating his body in a counterclockwise direction. His movements and the positioning of his body tell me he is about to throw a right low kick to the outside of my left thigh. Immediately I distribute my weight onto my right leg and begin lifting my left foot off the mat.

Staying balanced on my right leg, I elevate my left leg until my knee is at roughly the same height as my waist. Due to this action, Feijao's kick collides with the center of my left shin. My hands are up protecting my face, and I've kept my posture straight to ensure that I can quickly reestablish my fighting stance and launch a counterattack.

Rear Low Check Independent Movement (Standard Stance)

I've assumed a standard high stance.

I rotate my shoulders and hips in a counterclockwise direction.

I load my weight onto my left leg, straighten my posture, and begin to raise my right foot off the mat.

Staying balanced on my left leg, I lift my right leg until my knee is at roughly the same height as my waist. Notice how my leg is bent at about a ninety-degree angle and my knee is pointing toward my right side to ensure I check with the center of my shin.

CHECKING TECHNIQUES

PUSH CHECK

The push check is another block that can be used to combat your opponent's low to mid-range round kicks. The only difference between this technique and the standard check I demonstrated on the previous page is arm positioning. With the standard check, you keep both of your arms tight to your body and your hands elevated to protect your head. With the push check, you extend an arm and drive your hand into your opponent's torso or face. If you check with your left leg, you extend your right arm (Sequence A). If you check with your right leg, you extend your left arm (Sequence C). It's a bit more dynamic than the standard check, but it has several advantages. By extending your hand into your opponent's torso or face, you protect yourself from follow-up strikes. It also allows you to maintain distance, which prevents your opponent from engaging in the clinch upon throwing his kick. And if your opponent is within punching range when he throws his kick, it allows you to push his upper body backward, which throws him off balance, zaps the power from his kick, and sets you up for counterattacks.

(A) Block Right Round Kick with Lead Leg Push Check (Same Stance)

Feijao and I are both in a standard fighting stance, looking for an opening to attack.

As Feijao distributes his weight onto his lead leg and begins rotating his body in a counterclockwise direction, I prepare to defend against a low kick aimed at my lead leg by rotating my hips and shoulders in a counterclockwise direction, loading my weight onto my right leg, and extending my right arm toward his body.

Staying balanced on my right leg, I elevate my left leg so that my knee is at waist level and pointing toward my left side at a forty-five-degree angle. At the same time, I extend my right arm into Feijao's face. Notice that my left hand is up protecting my face, and my back is straight. From here, I will quickly reestablish my fighting stance and launch a counterattack.

(B) Rear Leg Push Check (Standard Stance)

1 I've assumed a standard fighting stance.

2 Protecting the right side of my head with my right arm, I extend my left arm straight out.

3 Staying balanced on my left leg, I elevate my right knee to waist level. Notice how my leg is bent at a ninety-degree-angle and my knee is pointing toward my right side.

(C) Block Left Round Kick with Rear Leg Push Check (Same Stance)

1 Feijao and I are both in a standard stance, searching for an opening to attack.

2 Feijao rotates his body in a clockwise direction, shifts his weight onto his right leg, and prepares to throw a left round kick at the outside of my right thigh. Immediately I rotate my hips and shoulders in a clockwise direction and extend my right arm toward Feijao's chest.

3 Shifting my weight onto my left leg, I elevate my right knee to waist level and extend my left hand into Feijao's face. Notice how my right arm is protecting the right side of my face and my back is straight. Having checked Feijao's kick with the center of my right shin, I will now quickly reestablish my fighting stance and launch a counterattack before he can recover from the kick.

REAR CROSS CHECK

When you execute a standard check, you block your opponent's right round kicks with your left leg and his left round kicks with your right leg. This is the ideal scenario because it allows you to retain your balance and quickly reestablish your fighting stance after the check is complete—both of which make it easier to immediately launch a counterattack. However, checking in this manner isn't always possible. Sometimes it can be difficult to spot a kick coming. Other times your positioning makes it difficult to check with the leg opposite to the one he's using to kick. When you can't utilize a standard check for whatever reason, your next best option is to employ a cross check. It makes it more difficult to immediately set up a counterattack, but it allows you to effectively block your opponent's kick, which should be your primary goal.

In the sequences below, I offer a few different versions of the cross check. First, I demonstrate the standard cross check, which is best utilized when your hips are square with your opponent's hips (Sequence A). The second cross check I offer involves employing a switch step before executing the check (Sequence B). This technique comes into play when your opponent circles around to the outside of your lead leg to acquire a dominant angle of attack, and then throws a round kick aimed at the outside of your lead leg. To protect yourself, you must handle your opponent's attack in two parts. By executing a switch step, you eliminate his dominant angle. One second he's to the outside of your lead leg, and the next second he's not. The downside is that when you execute the switch step, you place a larger portion of your weight onto your rear leg, which has now become your opponent's target. Instead of attempting to redistribute your weight to execute a standard check, which can take too much time, you utilize a cross check.

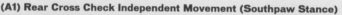

(A1) Rear Cross Check Independent Movement (Southpaw Stance)

1 I've assumed a southpaw high stance.

2 I rotate my hips and shoulders in a counterclockwise direction and load my weight onto my right leg.

3 Staying balanced on my right leg, I lift my left knee to waist level and sweep it across my body. It is important to notice that my left leg is bent at a ninety-degree angle, my hands are up protecting my face, and my back is straight.

(A2) Block Right Round Kick with Rear Leg Cross Check (Same Stance)

1

Feijao and I are both in a standard stance, looking for an opening to attack.

2

As Feijao prepares to throw a right round kick at my lead leg, I rotate my hips and shoulders in a counterclockwise direction and square my upper body with his.

3

As Feijao throws a right round kick at my lead leg, I elevate my right knee to waist level, sweep my leg across my body, and check his kick with the middle of my right shin. To stay balanced and maintain distance, I have extended my right arm. Notice how I am protecting the left side of my head with my left arm.

(B) Switch-Step Rear Cross Check

1

I've assumed a southpaw high stance.

2

I step my right foot behind my left foot to assume a standard stance.

3

Having switched my base, I lift my left knee to waist level and then sweep my leg across my torso to my right side. Notice how my left leg is bent at a ninety-degree angle, my posture is straight, and both of my hands are up to protect my face.

CHECKING TECHNIQUES

HIGH CHECK WITH DOUBLE-ARM BLOCK

When an opponent throws a round kick at your head, the choice method of defense is to either slip your head underneath his kick or quickly move out of range. However, if you're unable to evade his high kick due to your positioning or the quickness of his attack, the next best thing is to utilize a high check combined with a double-arm block. In the sequences below, I offer two variations of this technique, beginning with the standard high check with double-arm block. The checking part of this technique is the same as when you execute a low to mid-range standard check—the only difference is that you elevate your knee slightly higher. In the second sequence, I demonstrate how to execute a cross check double-arm block, which should be employed when you are unable to utilize the standard high check for whatever reason. Again, the checking portion is the same as the low to mid-range cross check, except here you elevate your knee slightly higher. In addition to increasing the elevation of your leg when you utilize both of these checks, you also want to employ a double-arm block with your arms. Early in the book I demonstrated how to perform an outside block using one of your arms to guard against your opponent's punches. When it comes to blocking kicks, guarding your head with one arm isn't enough. To reduce the impact, move your far arm across your torso and use it to help shield the side of your head. With both of your arms absorbing the blow, you not only reduce your chances of getting knocked out, but you also reduce the chance of breaking your arm. In the third sequence, I demonstrate how to execute a double-arm block without checking. Although this technique allows you to execute a speedier counterattack, it should only be used if you're absolutely sure your opponent's kick is aimed at your head, which can often be difficult to determine. Until you're a master at reading your opponent's kicks, I strongly suggest always using a check in conjunction with your double-arm block.

Rear High Check with Double-Arm Block Independent Movement (Southpaw Stance)

1

2

3

4

I've assumed a southpaw high stance.

I elevate my left arm to protect the left side of my head.

I move my right arm across my torso and to the front of my left arm. Notice how my palm is facing away from my body.

With my double arm block in place, I form a shield on my left side by elevating my left knee up to my left elbow.

Lead Cross Check with Double-Arm Block Independent Movement (Standard Stance)

1

I've assumed a standard high stance.

2

I elevate my right arm to protect the right side of my head.

3

I maneuver my left arm across my torso and position it in front of my right arm. Notice how my right palm is facing away from my body.

4

Having established my double-arm block, I form a shield on my right side by elevating my left knee and sweeping my leg across my torso to the right side of my body. From this position, I am protected from kicks aimed at either my head or midsection.

Double-Arm Block (Same Stance)

1

Feijao and I are in a standard high stance, searching for an opening to attack.

2

Feijao rotates his body in a counterclockwise direction to throw a right round kick at my head.

3

As Feijao throws a right round kick at my head, I reach my left hand behind my head, keep my left arm tight to the side of my face, and move my right arm across my torso and in front of my left arm. It is important to note that I'm absorbing the kick equally with both of my arms. If you absorb the impact on just one arm, the chances that you'll break your arm increase significantly.

STRIKING TECHNIQUES

STRIKING TECHNIQUES

In this section I break down the various strikes, including punches, elbows, kicks, and knees. When studying the moves, pay special attention to how each one is best utilized. Some strikes are more applicable as a lead-in attack, some work better as a secondary attack, and some are most effective as a counterattack. Later in the book I will demonstrate how to string various strikes together to form combinations, as well as show you how to use the various strikes to counter your opponent's attacks, but in the beginning it is best to focus on form and to learn the function of each strike.

PUNCHES

In this part of the section, I teach all the punching techniques that I use in mixed martial arts. No matter which punch you throw, you want to keep your striking arm relaxed and generate power using your legs, hips, and the rotation of your shoulders. If you have any tension in your arm, you will not only lose power and speed, but you'll also burn precious energy. It is also very important to immediately bring your striking arm back into your stance after landing a punch. A lot of fighters have the bad habit of dropping their arm as they bring it back toward their body, but if you're up against a good counterpuncher, this is an excellent way to get knocked out. To avoid breaking your hand, which is quite common in MMA due to the small gloves worn by the fighters, you always want to strike your target using only the knuckles of your index and middle fingers. To protect your face from counterstrikes, always keep your free arm elevated.

ELBOWS

This subsection includes all the elbow strikes that are common in both Muay Thai and MMA. First I cover the basic elbows that every MMA fighter should have in his arsenal, including side elbows, over-the-top elbows, and uppercut elbows. Next, I cover the more complex elbow strikes, including the reverse back elbow and the spinning back elbow. If you're new to striking, I suggest focusing on the basic elbow strikes because they are by far the most effective. Once you've mastered all the basic strikes, including punches, kicks, and knees, revisit the last portion of this section to beef up your arsenal with some flashy but effective moves.

KICKS

It is important to remember that mixed martial arts is not kickboxing. Due to your opponent's ability to take you to the mat, you have to be selective about how and when you kick. For example, when you throw a low roundhouse kick to your opponent's leg you are at less risk of being taken down than when you throw a mid-range roundhouse kick to his ribs. The reason for this is simple—mid-range roundhouse kicks have to travel a greater distance to reach the target and they are an easier kick for your opponent to catch. To be effective with mid-range kicks, you either want to set them up using other strikes such as punches or reserve them for when your opponent is hurt or backing up.

If your goal is to become a dangerous kicker, it is important not only to learn how to throw each kick fast and hard, but also understand how each kick makes you vulnerable. Once accomplished, you'll begin to spot situations where that vulnerability diminishes, allowing you to throw a particular kick with little to no risk. It is also important to learn the range in which each kick is best utilized, and if a kick can be utilized in multiple ranges, how you must adapt your form to minimize risk. A perfect example is the round kick. When in kicking range, you'll notice that I throw one arm down to generate power, but when I throw the same kick in punching range, I keep my hands up to protect myself from counterstrikes.

Another thing you must pay attention to is the target for each kick because it will often change according to your opponent's stance. For example, if you and your opponent have the same foot forward, you'll target the outside of his lead leg with a rear low round kick. However, if he places his opposite foot forward, your target will either be the inside of his lead leg or the outside of his rear leg.

It can take a long time to get your kicks to a level where you can use them effectively in competition. For this reason, I suggest focusing on the most basic and heavily utilized kicks first. This includes round kicks and front kicks. Once you get the hang of them, you can move on to the more dynamic kicks, such as the spinning back kick and the front up-kick.

JAB

The straight jab is one of the most important punches in mixed martial arts competition. It can be used to set up kicks, take-downs, and power punches. It can be used to close the distance between you and your opponent and establish the clinch. It's a phenomenal counterpunch, and it's also a phenomenal tool for preventing your opponent from bull rushing into your comfort zone. And unlike in boxing, you can cause a healthy amount of damage with a single jab, due to the small gloves worn by MMA combatants. If your goal is to have dangerous hands, I strongly suggest spending an ample amount of time developing this highly versatile punch and then exploring its various uses. In the sequence below, I demonstrate how to throw the straight jab from your stance, but it is important to mention that it can also be coupled with a step forward, a step backward, or even a side step to achieve a variety of goals.

1 Feijao and I have both assumed a southpaw stance. Notice how we are currently in striking range, which will allow me to throw a straight jab directly from my stance. If there were more distance between us, I would land the straight jab by throwing the punch and stepping forward at the same time.

2 Protecting the left side of my face with my left hand, I drive my right shoulder upward, extend my right arm straight out, and rotate my fist in a counterclockwise direction. It is important to notice that I haven't let my right elbow drift out to the side, which would considerably reduce the speed and power of my punch.

3 I drive off the mat with my rear foot to generate more forward momentum. At the same time, I continue to extend my right arm and rotate my fist in a counterclockwise direction, allowing me to strike my target with the knuckles of my index and middle fingers. Notice how my left hand is still protecting the left side of my face and my elevated right shoulder is protecting the right side of my jaw.

CROSS

The straight cross is one of the most feared weapons in mixed martial arts competition. When a competitor has mastered this strike, you'll often hear the commentators make such remarks as, "If he connects with his straight cross, the fight will be over." Landing a powerful cross to one of your opponent's vulnerable areas causes damage, plain and simple. But developing speed, power, and accuracy in your crosses doesn't happen overnight. It also takes a considerable amount of time to learn how to properly set up your crosses. Later in the book I demonstrate several combinations that can be used in tandem with the cross to increase its effectiveness, as well as how to use the cross as a counterpunch, but in the beginning it is important to focus on proper form. In the sequences below, I demonstrate the traditional right cross. In this version, the cross is thrown directly from your stance and is best utilized when you're already within striking distance of your opponent.

I've assumed a southpaw fighting stance.

Rotating my hips in a clockwise direction, I come up onto the ball of my left foot and throw my left fist straight out.

Continuing to rotate my hips in a clockwise direction, I turn my left fist over so that my palm is facing the mat and strike my target using the knuckles of my index and middle fingers. Notice how I have kept my right hand up and elevated my left shoulder to protect the left side of my face.

PUNCHES

SIDESTEP CROSS

In this sequence, I demonstrate the sidestep straight cross, which involves stepping your lead foot forward and to the outside as you throw the cross. In addition to allowing you to cover distance and create a more dominant angle of attack, your footwork also allows you to throw a more powerful and elusive strike. As with all the punches covered in this section, I recommend spending an ample amount of time each day drilling this technique. Throwing the sidestep cross while shadow boxing will increase your speed. Throwing it while hitting the heavy bag will develop power. And throwing it while striking the focus mitts and sparring will develop accuracy and a keen sense of timing and distance.

Sidestep Straight Cross (Same Stance)

1

Feijao and I are both in a southpaw stance, searching for an opening to attack.

2

I step my lead foot forward and toward my right side.

3

Having stepped my right foot to the outside of Feijao's rear foot, I place a larger portion of my weight onto my right leg, come up onto the ball of my left foot, rotate my body in a clockwise direction, and throw a left cross toward his face. Notice how I've kept my right hand up to protect the right side of my face.

4

I land a left cross to Feijao's chin, connecting with the knuckles of my index and middle fingers. Notice how I've elevated my left shoulder to protect the left side of my face from counterstrikes.

Sidestep Straight Cross (Opposite Stance)

Feijao and I are in opposite fighting stances. In order to acquire a dominant angle of attack in this scenario, I step my lead foot to the outside of his lead foot.

LEAD HOOK

When thrown correctly, the lead hook can be a very powerful punch, and because it approaches your target from the side rather than from straight on, it can also be a very difficult punch for your opponent to evade. Unlike straight punches, which can be slipped, the only way to avoid a hook is to move out of the way or duck underneath the punch, neither of which are easy to manage. Your opponent always has the option of blocking your lead hook with his arm, but it's not a very reliable option. Due to the small gloves worn in MMA and the circular path of your strike, your fist will often slip past his arm and connect with the side of his face. Possessing these positive traits, the hook is not a strike you want to overlook. To fully harness its potential, it is important to learn all the variations covered over the coming pages, as well as the situations in which each variation best applies. To begin, I've laid out two basic lead hook variations in the sequences below. The first is the standard lead hook. This punch is thrown using your entire body, and it is best employed when you're roughly an arm's length away from your opponent. The second variation is the lead close-range hook, which is best employed when in clinching range with your opponent. When studying the photographs and comparing these two techniques, pay special attention to the lower- and upper-body movements, as well as to hand and arm positioning. It is important to note that although I've only demonstrated these two strikes as lead-hand attacks, they can be thrown with your rear hand as well. Very little changes—your hand should follow the same circular trajectory, and your fist, elbow, and shoulder should all be on the same horizontal plane at the moment of impact. The only difference is that you pivot on your rear foot, rotate your body in the opposite direction, and throw the strike with your rear arm. With regard to range, the same rules apply. When you're in punching range, use the standard rear hook. When you're in clinching range, use the close-range rear hook.

Feijao and I are both in a southpaw stance, searching for an opening to attack.

I spot an opening to throw a lead right hook. Keeping my left hand up to protect the left side of my face, I rotate my hips and shoulders in a counterclockwise direction and extend my right arm outward along a circular path.

3

Continuing to rotate my hips and shoulders in a counterclockwise direction, I pivot on the ball of my right foot, rotate my fist so that my palm is facing the ground, and crash the knuckles of my index and middle fingers into the left side of Feijao's jaw. It is important to notice that my right fist, elbow, and shoulder have all traveled along a circular path on the same horizontal plane. It is also important to notice that I've shrugged my right shoulder to protect the right side of my jaw, as well as kept my left hand elevated to protect the left side of my face.

Lead Close-Range Hook Independent Movement

1

I've assumed a southpaw fighting stance.

2

Slightly rotating my hips and shoulders in a counterclockwise direction, I send my right fist along a tight circular path. Just as with the standard lead hook, I keep my fist, elbow, and shoulder on the same horizontal plane. However, instead of pivoting on my lead foot, I keep my toes pointing toward my opponent. And instead of turning my fist over so that my palm is facing the mat, I keep it vertical. To prevent injury to your hand, you want to strike your target with the knuckles of your index and middle fingers. To protect yourself from counterstrikes, shrug your right shoulder and keep your left hand elevated.

OUTSIDE SLIP TO LEAD POWER HOOK

In this sequence I demonstrate how to throw a lead hook off an outside slip. In addition to priming your hips for a more powerful punch, leading with the outside slip can also cause your opponent to react to your head movement, stealing his focus away from your punch that follows. Below I demonstrate the outside slip to lead hook as a lead-in attack, but it is important to note that this combination can also be utilized immediately after throwing a cross or to slip and counter one of your opponent's straight punches.

1

Feijao and I are both in a south-paw stance, searching for an opening to attack.

2

To execute an outside slip and load up for a lead right hook, I drop my level, come up onto the ball of my rear foot, rotate my hips and shoulders in a clock-wise direction, and dip my head toward my right side. Notice how I have kept my left hand up to protect my face from counter-punches.

3

Having executed an outside slip, I raise my elevation.

4

With my hips now spring-loaded from my clockwise rotation, I pull my left shoulder back, rotate my hips in a counterclockwise direction, and throw a right hook toward Feijao's face.

5

Still rotating my hips and shoulders in a counterclockwise direction, I pivot on the ball of my right foot, rotate my fist so that my palm is facing the ground, and crash the knuckles of my index and middle fingers into the side of Feijao's jaw. To protect myself from counterpunches, I have shrugged my right shoulder and kept my left hand positioned by the side of my face. It is important to notice that my right fist, elbow, and shoulder are all on the same horizontal plane.

DIAGONAL SWITCH-STEP TO LEAD HOOK

As you now know, switching your stance can be a clever way to confuse your opponent, throw off his defense, and create openings to attack. In the sequence below, I demonstrate how this simple footwork can be used to set up a rear hook. If you look at the photos, you'll notice that I begin the technique by taking a diagonal step forward with my back foot. Not only does this put me in an opposite stance, but it also provides me with a dominant angle of attack and exposes my opponent's jaw for a rear hook. Like the standard and lead power hook, the diagonal switch-step hook can be used as an attack, a counter to your opponent's straight punches, or as a secondary attack following a jab or cross. Below is an example of how the technique can be used as a straight-up attack, and later in the book I'll provide examples of how it can be used as a counterattack and a secondary attack.

Feijao and I are both in a southpaw fighting stance, searching for an opening to attack.

I step my left foot forward and toward my left side. This repositions my left foot to the outside of Feijao's lead leg and provides me with a dominant angle of attack.

Having slipped my head away from my centerline, I place a larger percentage of my weight onto my left leg, pivot on the ball of my right foot, rotate my hips and shoulders in a counterclockwise direction, and throw a right hook toward Feijao's face.

Continuing to rotate my hips and shoulders in a counterclockwise direction, I strike the side of Feijao's jaw with the knuckles of my index and middle fingers. To protect my face from counter punches, I have shrugged my right shoulder and kept my left hand up by my face.

OVERHAND

The overhand is responsible for putting countless fighters to sleep in mixed martial arts competition. The mechanics of the punch is similar to a straight cross, but instead of throwing your fist straight out, you drop your opposite shoulder and extend your arm forward in a downward arc, similar to a swimmer's freestyle stroke. Due to its arcing trajectory, your opponent can't slip the strike by moving his head away from his centerline, as can be done with straight punches. He can block the overhand with his arm, but it's not a very good option. If your hand slips through a crack in his protective shield, he will most likely go to sleep. And even when he manages to absorb the full impact with his arm, the power the overhand possesses will still cause him damage. Your opponent's best option when you throw the overhand is to quickly get out of the way, but by perfecting your timing and learning how to set up the strike, you can make that a difficult chore. If you overlook this strike, your arsenal will be lacking a very formidable weapon.

1

Feijao and I are both in a southpaw fighting stance, searching for an opening to attack.

2

Keeping my right hand up for protection, I come up onto the ball of my left foot, rotate my hips and shoulders in a clockwise direction, and slightly dip my right shoulder toward my right side.

3

Continuing to rotate in a clockwise direction and dip my right shoulder, I shift my weight forward.

4

As I rotate my body and dip my right shoulder toward my right side, I connect with the side of Feijao's face using the knuckles of my index and middle fingers. To protect myself from counterpunches I've not only shrugged my left shoulder and kept my right hand guarding my face, but I've also kept my head up and my eyes locked on Fred. If you drop your head or look at the ground, your ability to effectively follow up the overhand with another strike will decrease.

LEAD UPPERCUT

In the sequences below, I demonstrate two methods of throwing a lead uppercut. The first is a lead standard uppercut (Sequence A), which involves throwing the punch directly from your stance. It doesn't pack that much power, but it's a quick and elusive strike. In the second sequence I show the lead power uppercut (Sequence B). Before throwing the punch in this version, execute a slip by rotating your body and dropping your level. It's not as stealthy, but it packs a lot of power and is an excellent technique for slipping and countering one of your opponent's straight punches.

(A) Standard Lead Uppercut (Same Stance)

1

Feijao and I are both in a southpaw stance, searching for an opening to attack.

2

Keeping my left hand up to protect my face, I rotate my hips and shoulders in a counterclockwise direction.

3

Continuing to rotate my hips and shoulders in a counterclockwise direction, I distribute a larger portion of my weight onto my lead leg, come up onto the ball of my rear foot, turn my palm so that it is facing me, and throw my fist upward into Feijao's chin.

(B) Lead Power Uppercut (Independent Movement)

1
I've assumed a southpaw fighting stance.

2
Coming up onto the ball of my rear foot, I drop my right shoulder to generate power for the punch. Notice how my head has moved away from my centerline, which would have allowed me to avoid a punch directed at my face.

3
Pulling my left shoulder back, I whip my hips in a counterclockwise direction, rotate my hand so that my palm is facing me, and throw my fist upward. Notice how my left arm is up protecting my head.

4
I continue to rotate my body in a counterclockwise direction until my fist collides with my target. If you miss your strike or are shadow boxing in the gym, your fist should not come up past eye level.

PUNCHES

(B2) Lead Power Uppercut (Same Stance)

Feijao and I are both in a southpaw stance, searching for an opening to attack.

To generate power for the lead uppercut, I execute an outside slip by pivoting on my rear foot and rotating my body in a clockwise direction. Notice how I have reached my left hand behind my left ear to protect the side of my head.

Continuing to corkscrew my body in a clockwise direction, I load the majority of my weight onto my right leg and lower my elevation by bending at the knees and waist. Notice that I've dropped my right arm in preparation for the uppercut and kept my left arm elevated to protect the side of my head from my opponent's strikes.

Having spring-loaded my hips with my clockwise rotation, I pull my left shoulder back, whip my hips in a counterclockwise direction, and begin thrusting my fist upward toward Feijao's chin.

Continuing to rotate my hips and shoulders in a counterclockwise direction, I pivot on my right foot, rotate my right hand so that my palm is facing me, and thrust my fist upward into Feijao's chin.

PUNCHES

REAR UPPERCUT

Just as I did with the lead uppercut, I demonstrate two versions of the rear uppercut in the sequences below. First I cover the rear standard uppercut (Sequence A), a fast and sneaky punch thrown directly from your stance. Next, I demonstrate the power rear uppercut (Sequence B). This version can cause a lot of damage, but it is easier for your opponent to read due to your added movements. To increase its effectiveness, the rear power uppercut is best utilized after evading one of your opponent's straight punches using a quarter turn with inside slip. Later in the book I demonstrate how to plug the rear standard uppercut into a striking combination, as well as how to employ it as a counterattack, but in the beginning it is important to master the basic movements.

(A) Rear Standard Uppercut (Independent Movement)

1

I've assumed a southpaw fighting stance.

2

Pivoting on the ball of my rear foot, I rotate my hips in a clockwise direction, pull my right shoulder back, drop my left shoulder, and lower my left fist. Notice how I keep my right arm up to protect the right side of my face.

3

Still pulling my right shoulder back, I rotate my right hand so that my palm is facing me and throw my fist upward into my target.

(B) Rear Power Uppercut

1

Feijao and I are squared off in southpaw stances, searching for an opening to attack.

2

I step my right foot forward and toward my right side. As my foot touches down, I rotate my hips and shoulders in a counterclockwise direction, pivot on the ball of my right foot, and drop my left shoulder.

3

I raise my right arm to protect the right side of my head.

4

Having loaded my hips for the rear uppercut, I pull my right shoulder back, pivot on the ball of my left foot, and rotate my hips in a clockwise direction.

5

I shift my weight forward as I continue to pull my right shoulder back, pivot on my left foot, and rotate my hips in a clockwise direction.

6

Continuing with my previous movements, I rotate my left hand so that my palm is facing toward me and land a left uppercut to Feijao's chin.

CROSS STEP TO REAR UPPERCUT

In the footwork section, I demonstrated how to execute a simple cross step. Next, I covered how to use a cross step in conjunction with a slip to move out of the way of a straight punch and obtain a dominant angle of attack. Now, I show how a cross step can be used to acquire a dominant angle and set up a rear uppercut. In the sequence below, I demonstrate this technique as lead-in attack, but it is important to mention that it can also be used as a counterattack to combat your opponent's straight punches or in the middle of a striking combination.

Feijao and I are in southpaw fighting stances, searching for an opening to attack.

To obtain a dominant angle of attack, I execute a cross step by moving my right foot to the outside of Feijao's right foot. Notice that I have kept my right arm up to protect my head from strikes.

Pivoting on the ball of my left foot, I drop my left shoulder, pull my right shoulder back, and rotate my hips in a clockwise direction.

Continuing with my previous movements, I throw my left fist underneath Feijao's right arm and up into his chin.

SPINNING BACK FIST

The spinning back is a very powerful and sneaky punch that can be thrown with either your lead or rear arm. Although it can be employed as both an attack and a counterattack, it's not suitable for all situations. Having to turn your back to execute the punch, it's best to use it from a distance to prevent your opponent from stepping forward and wrapping you up as you rotate. Along these same lines, it is very important that you're quick with your movements so your back is exposed for only a short duration. In the blink of an eye, you want to make your rotation and strike. One of the nice things about this technique is you don't have to be as accurate as you do with other punches such as the cross and jab. You can strike your target with either your fist or forearm—both will cause damage. To demonstrate how this strike can be applied, I show how to throw the spinning back fist using your rear hand (Sequence A), and I show how to throw a spinning back fist using your lead hand to counter your opponent's cross (Sequence B).

(A) Rear Spinning Back Fist (Independent Movement)

1) I've assumed a southpaw stance. 2) I execute a right cross step. 3) Rotating my hips in a counterclockwise direction, I come up on the ball of my right foot and turn my head so that I can see my target out of the corner of my eye. 4) Still rotating my hips and shoulders, I whip my left arm in a counterclockwise direction along a horizontal plain, striking my target with either my fist or forearm.

(B) Counter Cross with Rear Spinning Back Fist (Opposite Stance)

Feijao is in a standard stance, and I'm in a southpaw stance. Both of us are looking for an opening to attack.

Feijao throws a right cross toward my face.

As Feijao's right cross comes at me, I step my right foot back, rotate my body in a clockwise direction, come up onto the ball of my left foot, and guide his right fist past me using my left arm.

Redirecting Feijao's right cross using my left hand, I step my left foot to the outside of his left foot and continue to rotate my body in a clockwise direction.

Still rotating in a clockwise direction, I step my right foot toward Feijao's left foot and elevate my right arm for the spinning back fist.

Using my footwork and clockwise rotation to generate power, I throw my right fist into the side of Feijao's head.

SIDE ELBOW

The side elbow follows the same circular path as a hook, but instead of striking your target with your fist, you make contact with the top portion of your forearm just below your elbow. In the sequences below, I demonstrate the lead and rear side elbow strikes, both of which can be employed when in the punching and clinching ranges of combat. However, when in punching or clinching range, your opponent will most likely have his arms up to protect his face. To land an effective side elbow, it's best to first disrupt his guard by leading with a knee strike or punches. If you manage to clear a path and land a side elbow clean, it can have devastating results. Below I demonstrate how to use both versions of the side elbow as a single-strike attack. To learn how they can be used in combinations, flip to the section devoted to attacks. To learn how they can be used to counter your opponent's hooks and side elbows, turn to the counterattacks section.

Lead Side Elbow (Independent Movement)

1

2

3

I've assumed a southpaw fighting stance.

Without moving my right hand, I elevate my right elbow, pull my left shoulder back, and rotate my hips and shoulders in a clockwise direction to generate power for the strike. Notice how I have kept my left hand up and my right elbow at jaw level to protect my face.

Rotating my hips in a counterclockwise direction, I pull my left shoulder back, thrust my right shoulder forward, and swing my right elbow along a circular path toward my target. Notice how my elbow doesn't extend past my chin. If you miss your target and overextend your strike, you leave yourself open for potential counterstrikes. To protect my face, I have kept my left hand up and my right elbow level with my jaw.

Lead Side Elbow (Same Stance)

Feijao and I are in southpaw fighting stances, searching for an opening to attack

Seeing an opening to throw a lead side elbow, I elevate my right elbow and step my right foot forward. At the same time, I drop my left shoulder and pull it slightly back, pivot on the ball of my lead foot, and rotate my hips and shoulders in a counterclockwise direction. Notice how I have kept my left hand up to protect my face.

Pulling my left shoulder back and rotating my hips in a counterclockwise direction, I thrust my right shoulder forward and throw my elbow along a circular path into Feijao's chin.

ELBOWS

Rear Side Elbow (Independent Movement)

1) I've assumed a southpaw stance. 2) Rotating my hips in a clockwise direction, I come up onto the ball of my left foot and elevate my left elbow so that it is on the same horizontal plain as my shoulder. 3) Continuing to rotate my hips in a clockwise direction, I thrust my left elbow along a circular path into my target. Notice how my left hand, elbow, and shoulder are all on the same horizontal plain. Also notice how I have kept my right hand up to protect my face from counterstrikes.

Rear Side Elbow (Same Stance)

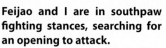

Feijao and I are in southpaw fighting stances, searching for an opening to attack.

2

In one fluid motion, I elevate my left elbow until it's level with my target, take a small outward step with my lead foot, slightly drop my right shoulder and pull it back, pivot on the ball of my rear foot, rotate my hips and shoulders in a clockwise direction, and throw my left elbow along a circular path toward Feijao's chin. Notice how taking a small outward step with my lead foot has allowed me to throw my elbow between Feijao's arms.

3

Continuing to pull my right shoulder back and rotate my hips in a clockwise direction, I thrust my left shoulder forward and strike Feijao's chin with the tip of my left elbow.

OVER-THE-TOP ELBOW

While the side elbow follows a horizontal path and often gets hung up on your opponent's arms, the over-the-top elbow reaches over your opponent's guard and crashes down on his head, making it a very difficult strike to block. Over-the-top elbows aren't as powerful as side elbows, but they have their advantages. The majority of the time, the tip of your elbow will glance off your opponent's forehead or eye socket, tearing the skin. Although there aren't many knockouts that can be attributed to an over-the-top elbow, it has produced more cuts than all other strikes combined. Like the side elbow, it can be employed from both the punching and clinching ranges of combat. It's also an excellent strike to utilize when in your opponent's guard.

Lead Over-the-Top Elbow (Independent Movement)

I've assumed a southpaw fighting stance.	Slightly rotating my body in a clockwise direction, I elevate my right elbow above my target and drop my left shoulder. Notice how I've kept my left hand up to protect my face.	Pulling my left shoulder back, I rotate my hips and shoulders in a counterclockwise direction, push my right shoulder forward, and throw my right elbow along a downward arc toward my target.	Continuing with my previous actions, I strike my target with the tip of my right elbow. To protect my face, I have kept my left hand up and shrugged my right shoulder.

Lead Over-the-Top Elbow (Same Stance)

Feijao and I are in southpaw fighting stances, searching for an opening to attack.

I begin my attack by elevating my right elbow, dropping my left shoulder, coming up onto the ball of my left foot, and rotating my hips and shoulders in a clockwise direction.

ELBOWS

Pulling my left shoulder back, I rotate my hips in a counterclockwise direction, push my right shoulder forward, and throw my right elbow along a downward arc toward Feijao's face.

Continuing with my previous actions, I strike Feijao's jaw with the tip of my right elbow. Notice how I have kept my left hand up to protect against counterstrikes.

Rear Over-the-Top Elbow (Independent Movement)

I've assumed a southpaw fighting stance.

Dropping my right shoulder and pulling it slightly back, I elevate my left elbow above my target, pivot on the ball of my rear foot, and rotate my hips in a clockwise direction.

Continuing with my previous actions, I throw my left elbow along a downward arc and strike my target. To protect my face, I have kept my right hand up and shrugged my left shoulder.

ELBOWS

UPPERCUT ELBOW

The uppercut elbow can be thrown a couple of different ways. In the first sequence below, I demonstrate how to throw the strike vertically into your target. It requires very little hip, shoulder, and arm movement, making it a very quick strike that works great for kick starting a combination, but due to the fact that it relies solely on the upward momentum of your arm, it doesn't pack much power. Next, I demonstrate how to throw the uppercut elbow along a diagonal path. This requires you to reach your striking arm across your face, as well as to employ hip and shoulder movement. It's a much more powerful strike that will likely result in a knockout rather than a cut, but it takes longer for your to elbow to reach your target, making it easier for your opponent to spot coming. Choosing which strike to employ will largely depend upon your personal preference and the situation you're presented with.

Lead Vertical Uppercut Elbow (Independent Movement)

I've assumed a southpaw fighting stance.

Drawing my right hand toward my right ear, I elevate my right elbow vertically and shift my weight onto my lead leg.

Using my forward shift to generate momentum, I draw my right hand toward the back of my head and throw my right elbow straight upward into my target. To protect my face, I have kept my left hand up and shrugged my right shoulder above my jaw.

Lead Diagonal Uppercut Elbow (Same Stance)

Feijao and I are in southpaw stances, searching for an opening to attack.

I move my right leg forward and plant on the ball of my foot. Next, I pivot on my right foot, rotate my hips and shoulders in a counterclockwise direction, and move my right hand toward the left side of my face.

Distributing a larger portion of my weight onto my right leg, I pull my left shoulder back, draw my right hand toward my left ear, and cast my right elbow along an upward, diagonal path into Feijao's chin.

Rear Vertical Uppercut Elbow (Same Stance)

Feijao and I are in southpaw stances, searching for an opening to attack.

Coming up onto the ball of my rear foot, I rotate my hips and shoulders in a clockwise direction, shift my weight onto my lead leg, and begin throwing my left elbow straight upward toward Feijao's chin.

Continuing to shift my weight onto my lead leg and rotate my hips and shoulders in a clockwise direction, I draw my left hand toward my left ear, drop my right shoulder, and strike Feijao's chin with the tip of my left elbow.

ELBOWS

DOWNWARD ELBOW

Although the downward elbow will probably be your least utilized elbow strike, it can have devastating results when executed with proper form and at the right moment. To pull it off, draw your arm behind your head and then drive the tip of your elbow downward into your opponent's face or skull. Even if you never find yourself in a situation where you can utilize the downward elbow from the standing position, it can still prove to be a valuable tool when lying on your back with an opponent in your closed guard. In my UFC fight against Travis Lutter, I trapped his head and arm between my legs in a triangle choke, and then forced a referee stoppage by landing repeated downward elbow strikes to his head. I'm not going to claim that it's a weapon you can't do without, but it's certainly a nice strike to have in your arsenal.

Lead Downward Elbow (Independent Movement)

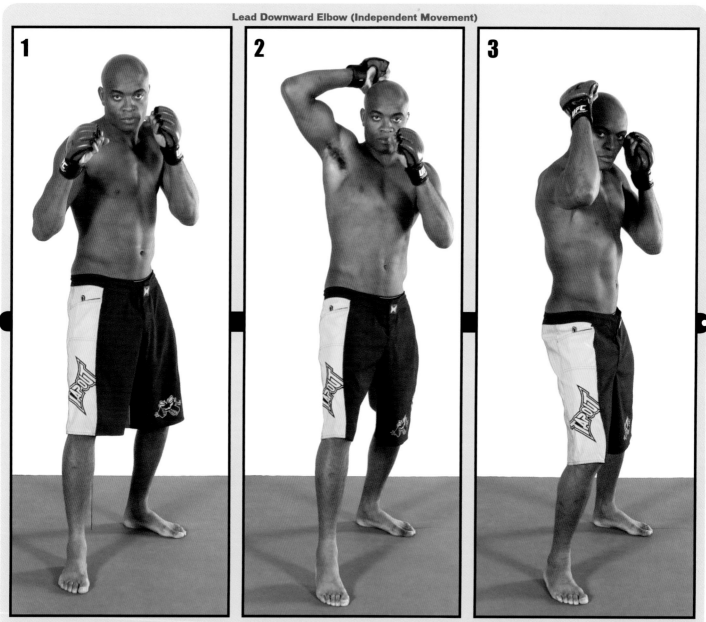

1) I've assumed a southpaw stance. 2) Keeping my left arm up for protection, I reach my right hand behind my head and elevate my right elbow to eye level. 3) Rotating my hips in a counterclockwise direction, I drive my right elbow downward into my target.

Lead Downward Elbow (Same Stance)

Feijao and I are in southpaw stances, searching for an opening to attack.

I come up onto the balls of my feet, rotate my hips and shoulders in a clockwise direction, and pull my right hand above my head. Notice how I angle my right elbow toward my right side.

Shifting my weight onto my lead leg, I twist my body in a counter-clockwise direction and throw my right elbow downward into the side of Feijao's jaw.

LEAD REVERSE BACK ELBOW

Not long before my Cage Rage fight with Tony Fryklund, I saw the movie *Ong Bak*. Tony Jaa, the martial arts hero in the movie, is a master at Muay Boran, an art I have always been interested in. There was one move he did in particular that blew me away. Instead of attacking with a side elbow or an over-the-top elbow, both of which are common in Muay Thai, Jaa stepped toward one of the villains and threw a lead reverse back elbow. I was so enamored with the move I went to my trainers and told them that I was going to use the strike in my next fight to knock out my opponent. Immediately they shut the idea down. "That won't work," they said. "Just forget about that elbow." I wasn't convinced, but every time I tried to practice the move during training, they could come running over and tell me to focus on techniques that would actually work.

I still wasn't convinced, so one night I went home and asked my wife to stand on the couch and hold out her hand. I executed a lead reverse back elbow into her palm, and she told me what I already knew—it was a very painful strike. To get in the practice I needed, I had her stand on the couch every evening after my official training—this time holding a pillow—and I would do one hundred lead reverse back elbows. By the time the Fryklund fight came around, I felt very confident. Unfortunately, backstage I couldn't sneak off with my wife to warm up on a pillow, so I had one of my training partners hold out a mitt so I could squeeze in a few more lead reverse back elbows. Again my trainers told me to forget that move. I figured I had no other choice but to prove them wrong, so two minutes into my fight with Fryklund, I stepped toward him, threw a lead reverse back elbow at his chin, and knocked him out.

I now use the lead reverse back elbow as a lead-in attack, a secondary attack, and as a counterattack. To set it up, you want to execute a lead quarter step with an inside pivot, which makes it look as though you're turning your back to your opponent. Once in position, drive your elbow upward into his face. When thrown correctly, it's a very deceptive strike because your movements make it look as though you are setting up a powerful rear strike instead of a lead hand strike. It's also a very difficult strike for your opponent to defend against because your elbow slips upward between his arms. It's a bit difficult to develop the timing and sense of distance needed to land the lead reverse back elbow, but when you put in the proper effort during training, it can yield spectacular results in a fight.

1

Feijao and I are in southpaw stances, searching for an opening to attack.

Coming up onto the ball of my lead foot, I rotate my hips and shoulders in a counterclockwise direction so that my right side is facing Fred. At the same time, I drop my right arm in preparation for the elbow strike. Notice how I position my left hand in front of my face to guard against punches.

Dropping my elevation by bending at the knees, I draw my right hand toward my left hip to generate power for the elbow strike.

I shift my weight onto my lead leg and then use that momentum to throw my right elbow upward into Feijao's jaw. It is important to notice that I have kept my left hand up to protect myself from punches.

ELBOWS

SPINNING REVERSE BACK ELBOW

In the previous sequence I demonstrated how to pull off a lead reverse back elbow by executing a lead pivot step, turning your lead shoulder toward your opponent, and driving your elbow upward into his chin. In this sequence, I show how to throw a rear reverse back elbow using a different setup. Instead of launching the strike directly from your stance, you step your lead foot to the outside of your opponent's lead leg, spin your whole body around, and then throw your elbow upward into his face. It requires you to momentarily turn your back to your opponent, which can make you vulnerable to takedowns, body locks, chokes, and strikes when utilized at the wrong moment, but it can have very favorable results when your timing is correct. By rotating your entire body in a circle, you not only generate a lot of power behind the strike, but your movement will also sometimes throw your opponent off and cause him to drop his guard or react in such a way that allows your strike to go unchecked. As with all spinning attacks, I recommend using them with extreme caution. If you feel the risks are greater than the potential reward, it is best to employ a lower-risk, higher-percentage attack.

Spinning Reverse Back Elbow (Independent Movement)

1) **I've assumed a southpaw stance.** 2) **I execute a cross step with my right foot and elevate my right arm for protection.** 3) **I rotate in a counterclockwise direction, come up onto the ball of my right foot, and drop my left arm in preparation for the spinning reverse back elbow.** 4) **Continuing to rotate in a counterclockwise direction, I step my left foot toward my imaginary opponent and drive my left elbow upward into his jaw.**

Spinning Reverse Back Elbow (Same Stance)

Feijao and I are in southpaw stances, searching for an opening to attack.

To execute a spinning back elbow, I first must acquire a dominant angle of attack. To accomplish this, I step my right foot to the outside of Feijao's right foot. To protect my face from strikes, I elevate my right arm.

Pivoting on the ball of my right foot, I spin my body in a counterclockwise direction until my left side is facing Fred. Notice how I have rotated my head to keep my eye on my target.

With Feijao's chin in my sights, I step my left foot to the inside of his right foot to close some distance between us, drop my right shoulder, and extend my left elbow upward into his chin. It is important to note that if you hesitate while your back is facing your opponent, he will be able to capitalize on your awkward positioning.

ELBOWS

SPINNING BACK ELBOW

The spinning back elbow is very similar to the previous technique. To set it up, you want to step to the outside of your opponent's lead leg, spin your body in a circle, and then throw an elbow at his face using your rear arm. However, instead of driving your elbow upward between your opponent's arms to collide with his chin, you throw it horizontally and collide with the side of his jaw. In the second sequence below, I demonstrate how to trap your opponent's arm while executing your rotation to clear a path for your strike. It is important to note that the arm trap can also be used in conjunction with the reverse spinning back elbow.

Spinning Back Elbow (Independent Movement)

1) I've assumed a southpaw stance.

2) I execute a lead cross step, come up onto the ball of my right foot, and begin rotating my body in a counter-clockwise direction

3) As I rotate my body, I elevate my right arm to protect my face from counterpunches.

4) Continuing to rotate in a counterclockwise direction, I pivot on my right foot, turn my head, and lock on to my target out the corner of my eye.

5) Using the momentum generated by my rotation, I throw my left elbow horizontally into my opponent's jaw.

Arm Trap Spinning Back Elbow

Feijao and I are both in a southpaw stance, searching for an opening to attack.

Pivoting on my feet, I rotate my body in a counterclockwise direction and hook my right arm around Feijao's right wrist.

Continuing to rotate in a counterclockwise direction, I break Feijao's guard by pulling his right arm away from his face. Notice how I turn my head halfway through my rotation to keep my eye on my target.

Still rotating in a counterclockwise direction, I throw my left elbow horizontally into Feijao's jaw.

LOW REAR ROUND KICK

To be effective with low rear round kicks, you want to strike the sciatic nerve running down the outside of your opponent's leg using the middle portion of your shin. The ultimate goal is to turn your leg into a baseball bat that strikes its target at ninety miles an hour, which can be achieved through thousands of repetitions on the heavy bag and Thai pads. But even when you land such a kick, seldom will your opponent drop to the canvas. When in a fight, your opponent's adrenaline will be on overload, and the superficial pain caused by your first round kick to his leg will most likely be registered rather than felt. Do not let this discourage you. The low round kick is not designed to knock your opponent out—it is designed to slowly chop him down through repeated strikes. When you land a half dozen kicks to the same spot on your opponent's leg, he will begin to limp around the ring or cage. Unable to bend his leg without it collapsing, his forward attacks and overall movement will greatly diminish. As his motivation to fight dwindles, he will often become desperate, throwing wild punches and lurching toward you with uncommitted takedown attempts. As long as you keep your head, you can use his weakened state and lack of posture to set up attacks and land knockout blows.

TECHNICAL NOTE

The rear low kick is best utilized from the punching and clinching ranges of combat, and it can be thrown directly from your stance or coupled with a lead side step to obtain a desired angle of attack. To set up the kick from punching range, it's wise to pull your opponent's focus away from his lower body by leading with a punching combination aimed at his head. When in clinching range, a good setup is to tie your opponent up in the dirty boxing clinch, use your single collar tie to pull him off balance, and then as he stumbles to regain his base, drive a powerful low kick into his thigh. If you're outside of punching range, it's best to take a forward step before unleashing the low kick. If you misjudge your range and throw the kick from too far out, you risk striking your target with your foot, which can have devastating results when your opponent manages to check the kick with his knee or shin.

Low Rear Round Kick to Outside Lead Leg

Feijao and I are in southpaw fighting stances, searching for an opening to attack.

To get within striking range, I step my right foot forward and toward my right side. At the same time, I come up onto the ball of my left foot, cross my left arm in front of my face to guard against strikes, and rotate my body in a clockwise direction. It is important to notice that my lead foot is pointing toward my right side at a forty-five-degree angle. Not only does this provide me with a dominant angle of attack, but it also sets my hips up to throw a powerful kick.

Pulling my right shoulder back, I whip my hips in a clockwise direction, lean back to balance my weight and move my head outside of punching range, and throw a rear low kick into the outside of Feijao's lead leg. Notice how I've thrown my left arm behind me. This not only helps me counterbalance my weight, but it also adds speed and power to my kick.

Low Rear Round Kick to Inside Rear Leg

It is important to note that you can also strike the inside of your opponent's leg using the low rear round kick. As with the majority of strikes, your target will be determined by the stance you and your opponent have assumed. If both of you have the same foot forward, you can use the rear low kick to target the outside of his lead leg or the inside of his rear leg. If you and your opponent have opposite feet forward, then you can use the rear low kick to target the inside of his lead leg or the outside of his rear leg.

Feijao and I are both in a southpaw stance, searching for an opening to attack.

To get within striking range, I step my right foot forward and toward my right side. At the same time, I come up onto the ball of my left foot, elevate my left arm to guard against strikes, and rotate my body in a clockwise direction. It is important to notice that my lead foot is pointing toward my right side at a forty-five-degree angle. Not only does this provide me with a dominant angle of attack, but it also sets my hips up to throw a powerful kick.

Pulling my right shoulder back, I rotate my hips in a clockwise direction and throw a rear low kick to the inside of Feijao's rear leg. Having covered a lot of distance to land the kick, I am now in punching range and vulnerable to a number of different strikes. To protect myself, I keep my right hand up, and to maintain distance between my opponent and me, I extend my left arm forward.

LEAD CUT KICK

Although the lead cut kick is not as powerful as the rear round low kick, it has several handy applications. Driving your lead shin into the soft flesh of your opponent's inner thigh not only sends a jolt of pain shooting up his leg, but it can also throw him off balance. As your opponent takes a small outward step with his lead foot to maintain his base, he will often lower his hands and tilt forward, creating an opening to follow up with a secondary attack. In addition to this, the lead cut kick is also an excellent strike to halt your opponent's forward progression. With every cut kick you land, your opponent will become more and more hesitant to move forward, allowing you to take charge in the offense department.

Lead Cut Kick to Inside Lead Leg

Feijao and I are both in a southpaw stance, searching for an opening to attack.

To cover distance and generate power for a lead cut kick, I move my left leg forward and plant my foot so that my toes are pointing toward my left side at a ninety-degree angle in relation to my opponent. Notice how my left heel is lined up with my right ankle, forming a T shape with my feet. This positioning opens my hips and will allow me to throw a damaging kick to the inside of Feijao's lead leg.

Keeping both of my hands up to protect my face, I pull my left shoulder back and begin rotating my hips in a counterclockwise direction.

Pulling my left shoulder back, I whip my hips in a counterclockwise direction and throw a lead cut kick to the inside of Feijao's right thigh. To cause the most damage, I've targeted the area just above his right knee with my right instep.

Having thrown Feijao off balance by landing a lead cut kick to the inside of his right leg, I immediately pull my right leg back toward my fighting stance.

I reestablish my fighting stance by dropping my right foot to the mat. Once accomplished, I can either use Feijao's compromised balance to launch a follow-up attack or step back to maintain distance. In this situation, I choose to step back.

Lead Cut Kick to Outside Rear Leg

When you and your opponent have the same foot forward, the majority of the time you'll want to throw the lead cut kick to the inner thigh of his lead leg, as demonstrated in the previous sequence. However, it is also possible to throw the lead cut kick to the outside of your opponent's rear leg. With your target further away, landing the kick requires you to move closer to your opponent, which makes you vulnerable to a number of counterattacks. It's not a kick you want to throw on a regular basis, but it certainly has its place. For example, if your opponent begins the fight in an opposite stance and you work his lead leg with rear round low kicks, a lot of times he will switch his stance to avoid taking any further abuse. With his injured leg now behind him, throwing lead cut kicks to his back leg can be worth the risks involved. The one thing you don't want to do with the lead cut kick is overcommit. Instead of generating power by dramatically rotating your hips and shoulders, you want to snap your shin into your target. If you should miss, this allows you to immediately reestablish your fighting stance and use footwork to move out of harm's way instead of exposing your back to your opponent.

Feijao and I are in southpaw stances, searching for an opening to attack.

I step my left foot forward. Because I'm attacking Feijao's rear leg, I take a slightly longer step than I would if I were throwing a cut kick to the inside of his lead leg. It is important to notice the positioning of my left foot when I plant it on the mat. My toes are pointing toward my left side, and my heel is pointing toward my right ankle. Positioning my foot in this manner opens my hips, which will allow me to throw a faster and more powerful kick.

Pulling my left shoulder back, I whip my hips in a counterclockwise direction and throw a lead cut kick to the front of Feijao's left leg. To cause the most damage, I strike just above his left knee using my right instep. To maintain distance and protect myself from strikes, I have kept my left arm up and extended my right arm into Feijao's body. From here, I will reestablish my fighting stance and either immediately follow up with another attack or back away and plot my next move.

MID-RANGE ROUND KICK

Throwing a round kick at your opponent's midsection is a lot more dangerous in MMA competition than it is in a Muay Thai bout. In both sports your opponent has the option of catching your kick with his arm and then using your awkward positioning to launch an attack, but in MMA he has the added bonus of being able to execute a takedown. For this reason, low round kicks are a lot safer and more heavily utilized. However, mid-range round kicks certainly have their place. If your opponent is off balance and in no position to catch your kick, driving your shin into his ribs can have devastating results. In addition, throwing round kicks at your opponent's midsection is also an excellent way to set up a high kick. For example, if you throw a mid-range round kick and your opponent drops his arm to catch your leg, you can pretty much assume he will do it again. The next time you throw a round kick, target his head instead of his ribs. Even for seasoned strikers, it can be very difficult to tell the difference between the two. If your opponent reads the trajectory of your leg wrong, the chances are he will shortly be taking a nap on the canvas.

Mid-Range Rear Round Kick

1 Feijao and I are in southpaw stances, searching for an opening to attack.

2 Rotating my hips and shoulders in a clockwise direction, I come up onto the ball of my left foot. To open my hips for a quick and powerful kick, I've pointed the toes of my right foot at a forty-five-degree angle toward my right side.

3 Distributing a larger portion of my weight onto my right leg, I posture up and prepare to throw a rear round kick to Feijao's midsection.

4 Pulling my right shoulder back, I whip my hips in a clockwise direction and throw a round kick to Feijao's midsection, connecting with the middle of my shin. Notice how I have kept my hands up to protect my face and leaned back slightly to maintain my balance.

Mid-Range Lead Round Kick

When in punching or clinching range, the mid-range lead roundhouse kick can be thrown directly from your fighting stance. It's not a very powerful strike, but it's quick, difficult to spot, and can be an excellent tool to hinder your opponent's forward progression. However, if your goal is to cause serious damage or you need to cover some distance to connect with your target, it's best to set up the kick by stepping your rear leg forward as demonstrated in the sequence below. If you look at the photos, you notice that with this particular strike I crash my shin across my opponent's abdomen instead of into his ribs.

Feijao and I are in southpaw fighting stances, searching for an opening to attack.

With Feijao having the same stance as me, I need to cover a good amount of distance to land a lead round kick to the left side of his midsection. To close the gap, I take a diagonal step forward with my left foot. To open my hips for a powerful kick, I position my left foot so that my toes are pointing toward my left side.

Distributing a larger portion of my weight onto my left leg, I pull my left shoulder back, rotate my hips in a counterclockwise direction, and come up onto the ball of my right foot.

Continuing to pull my left shoulder back and rotate my hips in a counterclockwise direction, I throw my right arm down to generate power for the kick and maintain balance, and launch a right round kick into Feijao's abdomen. To cause the most damage, I connect with the middle of my shin. To protect my face from counterstrikes, I have kept my left hand up.

HEAD KICK

The goal with the head kick is to catch your opponent with his hands down and crash your shin into his chin, the side of his neck, or the top portion of his head. Landing a head kick clean can instantly drop your opponent, but it can be a difficult strike to set up, especially when your opponent knows you have mean high kicks in your arsenal. As with mid-range round kicks, your opponent has the ability to catch your head kick and do all kinds of nasty stuff, making it a very important strike to setup. A good approach is to lead with strikes that target your opponent's lower extremities to pull his focus away from his upper body, and then follow up with a kick to his head. It's also an excellent strike to use when disengaging from the clinch. A lot of fighters have the bad habit of dropping their hands when they break from a tie-up position, allowing you to catch them before they reestablish their fighting stance. To keep your opponent guessing, it's important to mix up your high and mid-range kicks. If the first kick you throw is aimed at your opponent's skull, he'll be more hesitant to try and catch a kick aimed at his ribs. If the first kick you throw is aimed at his ribs, he'll be more likely to drop his arm when you throw a kick at his head. When deciding whether or not to throw a head kick, it is also important to read your opponent's energy level. If he is tired and his hands are heavy, his reactions will be a lot slower, making it easier to land a head kick flush.

Rear Head Kick

Feijao and I are in southpaw stances, searching for an opening to attack.

Distributing a larger portion of my weight onto my right leg, I come up onto the ball of my left foot and begin rotating my hips in a clockwise direction.

Keeping my posture erect, I throw my left arm behind me to counterbalance my weight, whip my hips in a clockwise direction, rotate on the ball of my right foot, and throw a left round kick to Feijao's chin and the side of his face. To guard against counterstrikes, I have kept my right arm elevated.

Lead Head Kick

Just like the lead low round kick, the lead head kick can be thrown directly from your stance. It's a sneaky and speedy strike that can catch your opponent off guard, but it doesn't have much in the power department. If your goal is to knock your opponent out, you'll want to first step your rear foot forward as demonstrated below. The added step allows you to close more distance and generate a whole lot more power with your hips and shoulders.

Feijao and I are in southpaw stances, searching for an opening to attack.

To establish the range needed to land a head kick with my lead leg, I take a diagonal step forward with my left foot. To open my hips for a powerful kick, I point the toes of my left foot toward my left side.

Pulling my left shoulder back, I whip my hips in a counterclockwise direction, throw my right arm down to generate power and counterbalance my weight, and launch a right round kick to the side of Feijao's head. To protect my face from possible counterpunches, I have kept my left arm elevated.

LEAD FRONT KICK

The lead front kick is similar to the boxers' jab in that it can be used to gauge distance, set up secondary attacks, and stop an advancing opponent. To be effective with the strike, begin by lifting your knee straight up toward your chest. Once accomplished, extend your leg outward, thrust your hips forward, and strike your target with the ball of your foot. In the first sequence below, I demonstrate how to throw the lead front kick to your opponent's solar plexus. This is the most common target because it allows you to thwart your opponent's attack, knock the wind out of him, and force him backward, which often creates an opening for a secondary attack. In the second sequence, I show how to target your opponent's lead hip. Although it doesn't cause the same type of damage, it is an excellent strike for thrusting your opponent off balance without pushing him backward, which creates an opportunity to follow up with a close-range attack such as a punch or another kick. In the last sequence, I demonstrate how to target your opponent's lead leg. If you look at the photos, you'll notice that as I land the kick, my opponent's lower body gets forced backward, causing his head to drop. Such a strike is excellent for setting up knees to the midsection or face. No matter which target you choose, it is important to retract your leg and reestablish your fighting stance before moving on to your next attack. A common mistake a lot of fighters make is they overcommit to the kick and fall forward directly into a punch. As long as you spend time each week practicing proper form, such a scenario can be easily avoided.

Lead Front Kick to Solar Plexus

Feijao and I are in southpaw stances, searching for an opening to attack.

To generate power for the kick, I lift my right knee toward my chest and lean back slightly.

Thrusting my hips forward, I drive the ball of my right foot into Feijao's solar plexus. Notice how I have maintained my balance on my left foot. If you miss your kick and your balance is off, you'll most likely fall forward or backward and be vulnerable to counterattacks.

Lead Low Front Kick to Hip

Feijao and I are in southpaw fighting stances, searching for an opening to attack.

I lift my right foot straight up off the mat.

Without leaning backward, I thrust my hips forward and drive my right foot into Feijao's lead hip. With his base and balance compromised, I will immediately follow up with a secondary attack.

Lead Low Front Kick to Knee

Feijao and I are in southpaw fighting stances, searching for an opening to attack.

To generate power for the kick, I elevate my right knee toward my chest and lean back slightly.

Thrusting my hips forward, I lean back to maintain my balance and thrust the ball of my right foot into Feijao's right knee, causing him to bend forward. With his posture compromised, I will immediately follow up with a secondary attack, such as a knee to the face.

REAR FRONT KICK

The rear front kick is more powerful than the lead front kick, but it is slower and easier for your opponent to spot due to the distance your leg has to travel. Like the lead front kick, it can be used as an attack, in combination with other strikes, and as a counter to halt your opponent's forward progression. Its dynamics are also similar in that you want to lift your knee toward your chest before extending your leg and thrusting your hips forward. However, there are two different methods for recovering after throwing the kick. You can retract your leg and reestablish your original fighting stance, or you can switch your stance by dropping your striking foot to the mat in front of you. The former allows you to maintain distance between you and your opponent and follow up with strikes from the mid-range of combat, and the latter allows you close the distance and either tie your opponent up in the clinch or attack with a close-range combination. Deciding which option to utilize should be based upon the situation and your goals in the fight.

1

Feijao and I are in southpaw stances, searching for openings to attack.

2

Rotating my hips and shoulders in a clockwise direction, I lift my left foot off the mat and draw my knee toward my chest.

3

Having elevated my left knee, I drive the ball of my left foot into Feijao's abdomen.

4

As I extend my left leg and drive the ball of my foot into Feijao's abdomen, I lean back to maintain my balance. Notice how my strike has not only pushed Feijao backward, but also disrupted his balance. From here I can either reestablish my fighting stance (Fig. A) or drop my left foot to the mat, establish a standard fighting stance (Fig. B), and immediately follow up with a secondary attack.

5 (A)

Resume Fighting Stance

Switch Stance (B)

(A) **Resume Fighting Stance:** Having landed a stiff rear front kick to Feijao's abdomen, I rotate my hips and shoulders in a counterclockwise direction, pull my left leg behind me, and reestablish a southpaw stance.

(B) **Switch Stance:** Having landed a hard rear front kick to Feijao's abdomen, I decide to capitalize on his compromised positioning by switching to a standard fighting stance, which is accomplished by dropping my left foot and planting it on the mat in front of me. By taking this action, I am now within range to immediately follow up with a punch, kick, knee strike, or takedown. However, even if you plan on switching your stance prior to throwing the kick, it is important that you don't lean into your strike because if you should miss, it will cause you to fall forward. And if you fall forward, you'll be left in a compromising position and be vulnerable to counterattacks.

FRONT STOMP KICK

The stomp kick has a very appropriate name. It's similar to the front kick in that you begin by drawing your knee toward your chest, but instead of shooting your leg straight forward and striking with the ball of your foot, you angle your knee off to the side and extend your leg at a downward angle, stomping your entire foot into either your opponent's hip or knee. If you land the kick clean, your opponent will bend forward at the waist and most likely drop his guard, opening an array of attacking options such as a straight knee or head kick. However, due to the downward angle of attack, the technique tends to work best on opponents who are shorter or the same height as you.

Lead Stomp Kick (Opposite Stance)

The lead stomp kick is best utilized when you and your opponent are squared off in opposite fighting stances, and the ideal target is your opponent's lead hip. If you and your opponent have the same feet forward, you'll want to employ the rear stomp kick demonstrated in the following sequence.

Feijao has assumed a standard fighting stance, and I've assumed a southpaw fighting stance. Both of us are searching for an opening to attack.

To generate power for a lead stomp kick, I shift my weight onto my left leg and draw my right knee toward my chest.

To throw the stomp kick, I point the toes of my right foot at a forty-five-degree angle toward the ceiling, thrust my hips forward, and drive my entire foot into Feijao's left hip. It is important to notice that the angle of my right foot allows me to strike my target with my entire sole. The force of the blow forces Feijao to tilt forward at the waist. From here, I can capitalize on his compromised positioning by following up with a secondary attack.

Rear Stomp Kick to The Hip

The rear stomp is best utilized when you've assumed the same fighting stance as your opponent. The kick packs more power than the lead stomp kick, but it is easier for your opponent to see it coming due to the distance your leg has to travel. With this strike, you can target either your opponent's lead hip or knee.

Feijao and I are in southpaw stances, searching for an opening to attack.

To generate power for a rear stomp kick, I lift my left knee toward my chest. Notice how I have angled my knee toward my left side.

I point the toes of my left foot toward the ceiling at a forty-five-degree angle, thrust my hips forward, and drive my left foot at a downward angle into Feijao's right hip. Having struck my target with my entire sole, Feijao is forced to tilt forward at the waist. To capitalize on his compromised positioning, I will immediately follow up with a secondary attack.

Rear Stomp Kick to The Knee

Feijao and I are in southpaw fighting stances, searching for an opening to attack.

To generate power for a stomp kick, I lift my left knee toward my chest. Notice how I have angled my knee toward my left side.

Angling the toes of my left foot toward my left side, I thrust my hips forward and drive my foot at a downward angle into the soft area just above Feijao's right knee. Having struck my target with my entire sole, the impact forces Feijao to tilt forward at the waist, creating an opening for me to follow up with another attack.

KICKS

FRONT UP-KICK

The front up-kick is a deceptive and difficult strike to block. The downside is that it's also a difficult strike to throw. In order to pull it off, you must cross your lead leg to the opposite side of your body and then launch it in an upward arc, kind of like a kung-fu back fist. The goal is to sneak your foot between your opponent's arms and catch him square in the jaw. As long as you don't telegraph the type of strike you're throwing, your opponent will see your right foot move and immediately expect you to attack his left side. When your foot winds up between his arms and in his face, he won't know what hit him. It's a pretty advanced strike, so I suggest mastering the basic kicks such as the low round kick and the straight front kick before playing around with it, but once you've got the basics down, it's important to experiment as much as possible to discover what works best for you. If you try the front up-kick and find it as effective as I do, you might want to incorporate it into your bag of tricks. After all, the bigger your bag of tricks, the harder it will be for your opponent to predict your attacks. In the first two sequences below, I demonstrate how to throw the kick using your lead leg, and in the last two sequences I show how it can be executed using your rear leg.

Lead Front Up-Kick (Independent Movement)

1) I've assumed a southpaw stance.

2) I slide my left foot toward my right to cover distance, straighten my posture, and turn my body in a counter-clockwise direction.

3) As I lift my right foot off the mat, I cross my right knee toward the left side of my body.

4) Elevating my right knee, I whip my right foot upward and toward my right. Following this trajectory allows me to circle my leg around my opponent's arms and strike his face with my foot.

5) I come up onto the ball of my left foot and snap my right foot into my target.

Lead Front Up-Kick

Feijao and I are in southpaw stances, searching for an opening to attack.

To set up the kick, I execute an inside pivot by rotating my body in a counterclockwise direction, pivoting on my right foot, and circling my left foot behind my right.

I slide my left foot toward my right, come up onto the ball of my right foot, and angle my right knee toward my left side.

Coming up onto the ball of my left foot, I swing my right leg on a circular path around the outside of Feijao's body. Once I clear his right arm, I snap my foot into the right side of his face.

Rear Front Up-Kick (Independent Movement)

1

I've assumed a southpaw fighting stance.

2

Coming up onto the ball of my rear foot, I shift the majority of my weight onto my lead leg and rotate my hips and shoulders in a clockwise direction.

3

I slide my right foot up to my left, and then lift my left knee toward my chest.

4

As I throw my left knee upward, I whip my leg along a circular path toward my left side.

5

Coming up onto the ball of my right foot, I snap my left foot into my target.

Rear Front Up-Kick

Feijao and I are in southpaw stances, searching for an opening to attack.

Rotating my body in a clockwise direction, I come up onto the ball of my rear foot and shift a larger portion of my weight onto my lead leg. Notice how I have kept my left hand up to protect my face from counterstrikes.

Coming up onto the ball of my right foot, I circle my left leg around the left side of Feijao's body and then snap my foot into the left side of his face.

SIDE KICK

Check out any one of Bruce Lee's films and you'll see him throw a multitude of side kicks on a host of villains. He employed this technique often not only because it's beautiful to witness, but also because it's highly effective and packs a tremendous amount of power. However, landing the kick clean isn't as easy as Lee made it appear on the silver screen, especially when your opponent utilizes side-to-side movement. For the best results, the side kick should be employed when your opponent advances quickly toward you or when he retreats straight back. In both cases, your timing and sense of distance must be nail sharp. If your opponent is advancing and you allow him to close the distance, your leg will get bunched up. This not only removes all the sting from your kick, but it also sacrifices your base. If your opponent is retreating and you throw the kick too late, you'll have to overcommit to reach your target, which also sacrifices your base. The only way to get this kick down pat is to practice it over and over while sparring. Once you have the movements, timing, and sense of distance ingrained in your mind, you'll be able to send your opponent flying through the air, just like Lee did in his action flicks.

Lead Side Kick (Independent Movement)

1) I've assumed a southpaw stance. 2) I slide my left foot behind my right foot and then plant it on the mat in front of me. 3) I shift my weight onto my left leg, lift my right knee to my chest to generate power for the kick, and turn my body in a counterclockwise direction. 4) With my right knee elevated, I lean back to maintain my balance, thrust my hips forward, and extend my right foot straight out toward my target. 5) I drive my right foot into my imaginary opponent's midsection. Notice how my foot is perfectly horizontal and I have my eyes locked on my target.

Side Kick

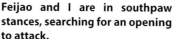

Feijao and I are in southpaw stances, searching for an opening to attack.

Sensing an attack, Feijao takes a step back. The instant he does this, I slide my left foot behind my right foot and plant it on the mat in front of me.

Feijao continues to move straight back, setting me up perfectly for a side kick. As he steps his left foot behind him, I distribute my weight onto my left leg and raise my right knee toward my chest.

With my right knee elevated, I lean back, thrust my hips forward, and throw a right side kick to Feijao's midsection. It is important to notice that I've remained perfectly balanced. If you lean too far forward or back and miss your kick, your balance and base will be compromised.

SPINNING BACK KICK

Landing clean with a spinning back kick is an excellent way to cause your opponent an extreme amount of pain and send him flying across the ring, but just as with all spinning attacks, it can be a very risky maneuver. Before executing this type of flashy attack, you must weigh the risks versus the potential rewards. You have to break down the variables. Does your opponent have the skill and energy to counter when you turn your back? What position will the technique land you in should you miss? And if you miss the strike and your opponent capitalizes on your poor positioning, will you be able to escape? Failing to compute these factors before throwing the kick might add a clip to your opponent's highlight reel instead of yours. If you don't think you could survive the worst-case outcome, utilize a safer technique.

Spinning Back Kick (Independent Movement)

1) I've assumed a southpaw fighting stance.

2) I execute a lead cross step and turn my body in a counterclockwise direction.

3) Still rotating my body in a counterclockwise direction, I come up onto the ball of my right foot and spin my head to keep an eye on my target.

4) To setup my hips for a powerful kick, I corkscrew my shoulders in a counterclockwise direction.

5) With my wound-up shoulders tugging my hips in a counterclockwise direction, I release that tension and throw my left foot straight into my target. To counter-balance my weight, I lean my upper body forward. It is important to notice that I generate power using the rotation of my body rather than driving my body toward my target. If you lean into your opponent and miss, your balance will be compromised, leaving you vulnerable to attack.

Spinning Back Kick

Feijao and I are in southpaw fighting stances, searching for an opening to attack.

Sensing an attack, Feijao steps his right leg back and begins to retreat out of punching range. The instant he does this, I generate power for a spinning back kick by pivoting in a counterclockwise direction so that my back is facing my opponent. Notice how I've also spun my head to keep my eye on my target.

Shifting my weight onto my right leg, I throw my left foot straight back into my target. To counterbalance my weight, I lean my upper body forward. It is important to notice that I generate power using the rotation of my body rather than driving my body toward my target. If you lean into your opponent and miss, you'll balance will be compromised, leaving you vulnerable to attack.

STRAIGHT KNEE

The straight knee is one of the most powerful strikes in your arsenal, and it is also one of the most versatile. It can be used when you establish double collar ties and secure the Muay Thai clinch (Figure A), and it can be used when you establish a single collar tie and secure the dirty boxing clinch (Figure B). The straight knee is also an excellent weapon to use both as an attack and counterattack when in punching range with your opponent. To effectively employ it as an attack while in punching range, it's best to first launch a combination that involves punches aimed at your opponent's face. This allows you to close the distance and overwhelm your opponent, which will usually cause him to defensively raise his hands to guard against your onslaught. The instant he covers up, drive straight knees into his vulnerable areas, such as his stomach, solar plexus, and ribs. To employ straight knees as a counterattack from punching range, it's best to wait until your opponent rushes haphazardly forward with strikes or drops his level and shoots in for a takedown. If your timing and sense of distance are sharp, your opponent will run straight into your knee strike and most likely drop to the canvas to take a nap.

In addition to being highly versatile, straight knees are also very difficult for your opponent to block for several reasons. First, it is a hard strike to see coming because it only has to travel a short distance, and it approaches along an upward trajectory. Secondly, it yields a tremendous amount of power. When your opponent spots a straight knee coming at him, the majority of the time he will instinctively attempt to block it with his arms only to have your knee blast through his guard like a battering ram. In the sequence below, I demonstrate how to throw both the rear and lead straight knee strikes. The rear knee is the more powerful of the two, and it can be thrown directly from your fighting stance (Sequence A) or coupled with a side step (Sequence B). With the latter, you change your angle of attack, which increases your chances of landing the strike unchecked. When throwing a straight knee with your lead leg, it's best to step your rear foot forward to break the distance and generate power for the strike. Once you've covered the necessary distance, throw your knee directly into your target. I suggest drilling both knees equally and as often as possible. The more comfortable you become with these techniques, the easier it will be to utilize them effectively in a fight.

Fig A: Muay Thai Clinch   Fig B: Dirty Boxing Clinch

(A) Rear Straight Knee

1

Feijao and I are in southpaw stances, searching for an opening to attack.

Keeping both of my hands up to protect my face, I rotate my hips and shoulders in a clockwise direction and come up onto the ball of my rear foot.

I straighten my right leg and thrust my hips forward.

Staying balanced on my right leg, I elevate my left knee and then drive it into Feijao's solar plexus using the forward momentum of my hips. From here, I can assume my original fighting stance by pulling my left leg behind me or I can drop my left foot straight down to the mat, assume a standard fighting stance, and engage Feijao in the clinch.

(B) Lead Side Step to Rear Knee

Technical Note: When you execute the lead side step in this technique, it spreads your legs apart and widens your base. In the footwork section, I discussed the important of never getting too spread out. In most cases you'd want to slide your rear foot toward your lead foot after executing the side step, but in this particular technique you want to immediately throw the knee strike. Not only does this make the strike quicker, but it also makes it more difficult for your opponent to defend against. However, to prevent from falling while throwing the knee strike, it is very important that you counterbalance your weight by dropping your rear shoulder, as demonstrated in the photos below.

I've assumed a southpaw stance.

I execute a lead side step by moving my right foot forward and toward my right side.

I drive off my left foot, distribute my weight onto my right leg, twist my body in a clockwise direction, drop my left shoulder to counterbalance my weight, and then drive my left knee upward into my target.

Lead Straight Knee

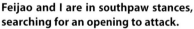

Feijao and I are in southpaw stances, searching for an opening to attack.

To close the distance between my opponent and me so that I'm within kneeing range, I step my rear foot forward. If you begin in punching range, slide your rear foot up to your lead foot, as demonstrated in the photo on the right. If you begin outside of punching range, step your rear foot in front of your lead foot, as demonstrated in the photo on the left. In both cases, your forward momentum will add power to your strike.

Having closed the distance, I lift my right knee straight up.

Leaning back, I thrust my hips forward and drive my right knee straight into Feijao's solar plexus. With this knee strike, it is important to attack your target horizontally rather than vertically. In other words, lift your knee and then drive it forward rather than driving your knee straight up into your target. It is also important to notice that I've kept my hands up to protect my face. From here, I can reestablish my original fighting stance by bringing my right leg behind me or I can drop my right foot straight down to the canvas, assume a southpaw stance, and engage Feijao in the clinch.

KNEES

SIDE KNEE

Like the straight knee, the side knee can be utilized from both the punching and clinching ranges of combat, as well as thrown with either your lead or rear leg. It's not as powerful or versatile as the straight knee, but it can cause serious damage when thrown properly and at the right moment. To throw an effective side knee with your lead leg, take a diagonal step forward with your rear foot to break the distance and change your angle of attack. Once you acquire a dominant angle, target your opponent's solar plexus with your strike (Sequence C). Throwing a side knee with your rear leg can be done directly from your fighting stance, and you want to target your opponent's rib cage, just below his armpit. If you land clean with either strike, you'll most likely knock the wind out of your opponent, which can either end the fight right there or create an opening for you to follow up with more knees or another secondary attack.

If you look at the sequences below, you'll notice that the mechanics of the side knee are very similar to the mechanics of a round kick. There are two primary differences between the two strikes. The first has to do with form. With the side knee, you keep your leg bent at roughly a ninety-degree angle so that you strike your target with the point of your knee. With a round kick, you straighten your leg considerably more to insure that you strike your target with your shin. The second difference between the two strikes has to do with range. The round kick is thrown from kicking and punching distance, and the side knee is thrown from punching and clinching distance. However, with both you and your opponent moving about the cage or ring, range can change in a blink of an eye. As long as you are constantly aware of range, you can use the two strikes in conjunction with one another due to their similarities in form. For example, if you throw a round kick at your opponent's midsection and he quickly moves forward into clinching range to avoid the attack, instead of straightening your leg and following through with your kick, you can land a powerful knee strike by keeping your leg bent and driving your knee into his side. Along these same lines, if you throw a side knee and your opponent quickly retreats into kicking range to avoid the attack, you can straighten your leg and land a round kick. Although judging range and switching from one strike to another may seem easy, it requires nail-sharp timing and a keen sense of distance. These attributes can only be developed through countless hours sparring and hitting the focus mitts and Thai pads.

(A) Rear Side Knee (Independent Movement)

1) I've assumed a southpaw fighting stance.

2) I come up onto the ball of my left foot and rotate my hips and shoulders in a clockwise direction.

3) Shifting my weight onto my right leg, I drive off my left foot and elevate my left knee.

4) I swing my left knee along a circular path toward my target. Notice how I have leaned my upper body toward my right side to counterbalance my weight.

5) Continuing to rotate my hips in a clockwise direction, I keep my left leg bent at about a ninety-degree angle, throw my left arm behind me to counterbalance my weight and generate more momentum, pull my right shoulder back, pivot on my right foot, and throw my left knee upward along a diagonal trajectory into my target. Notice how I have kept my right hand up to protect my face.

(B) Lead Side Knee (Independent Movement)

1) I've assumed a southpaw stance. 2) To cover distance and generate power for a lead side knee strike, I step my rear foot forward. 3) The instant I switch my stance, I shift my weight onto my left leg and begin rotating my hips and shoulders in a counterclockwise direction. 4) Pushing off the ball of my right foot, I send my right knee along an upward arc toward my target. 5) Continuing to rotate my hips in a counterclockwise direction, I pivot on my left foot, throw my right arm behind me to counterbalance my weight, and strike my target with the tip of my knee. Notice how I have kept my left hand up to protect my face.

(C) Lead Side Knee

Feijao and I are in southpaw stances, searching for an opening to attack.

To generate power for the strike and obtain a dominant angle of attack, I step my left foot forward and to the outside of Feijao's right foot.

Having acquired a dominant angle of attack, I rotate my body in a clockwise direction and lift my right foot off the mat.

Latching on to the back of Feijao's right shoulder using my right hand, I rotate my body in a counterclockwise direction, curl my right heel toward my butt, and drive my right knee into his solar plexus. From here, I can drop my right foot straight down to the mat and tie Feijao up in the clinch, or I can disengage, place my right foot behind me, and establish a standard fighting stance.

Fig 1D: Lead Round Kick

Notice the similarities between the lead round kick and the lead side knee.

FLYING KNEE

If you've watched your share of MMA fights, then I'm sure you've seen a competitor get brutally knocked out as the result of eating a flying knee. Not only is the strike fast and powerful, but it is also a very difficult strike for your opponent to block when thrown at the right time and with proper technique. Like most knee strikes, it can be used as both an attack and a counter. The best way to set up a flying knee is to use footwork and strikes to force your opponent to back up. The instant he begins backpedaling, move forward, leap through the air, and throw a knee toward his body or head. The best time to use a flying knee as a counterattack is when your opponent drops his level to shoot in for a takedown. With his face moving toward your legs and your knee moving toward his face, an unobstructed collision will usually drop him to the canvas. This is exactly what happened when I fought Carlos Newton in the Pride Fighting Championships with a flying knee.

The downside is that flying knees are often risky to throw. The instant your feet come off the canvas, you're committed to the technique, which makes you vulnerable to counterstrikes and takedowns. Before utilizing flying knees, it is very important to ask yourself if the potential rewards are worth the risk. If your ground game is lacking and you're up against a strong wrestler or jiu-jitsu specialist, pulling a flying knee out of your bag of tricks might not be the wisest move. When I fought jiu-jitsu specialist Travis Lutter, I landed a flying knee clean, but he still managed to haul me to my back. I executed the technique because I was confident in my ground skills and knew I could survive the worst-case scenario. If you don't feel this is the case, then it's best to forgo spinning or flying techniques for something safer. Adding to your highlight reel is nice, but taking home a win is a whole lot nicer.

Flying Straight Knee Independant Movement

1) I've assumed a standard stance. 2) I drop into a low stance by bending at the knees and sinking my hips. 3) Leaping forward into the air, I scissor my legs and drive my knee into my target.

Flying Straight Knee

Feijao and I are in southpaw stances, searching for an opening to attack.

I drop into a low stance by bending at the knees and sinking my hips.

Leaping forward and into the air, I scissor my legs and drive my left knee toward Feijao's face.

Flying High Knee (Independent Movement)

In contrast to the flying straight knee, the high knee has an upward trajectory and is best utilized when in close range.

1

I'm in a southpaw stance.

2

I drop down into a low stance by bending my knees and sinking my hips.

3

I leap straight up into the air and scissor my legs.

4

I throw my left knee straight up into my target.

Flying High Knee

1

Feijao and I are in opposite stances, searching for an opening to attack.

2

I drop down into a low stance by bending at the knees and sinking my hips.

3

I leap straight up in the air, scissor my legs, and throw my right knee toward Feijao's face.

ATTACKS

ATTACKS

Having covered fundamental movement and striking techniques, it's time to put everything together into attacking combinations. With all the combinations I offer in this section, the ultimate goal is to turn your opponent's entire body into a target and strike from odd, unpredictable angles. As you already know, this can be accomplished by acquiring a dominant angle of attack. However, standing face-to-face with your opponent, it can be very difficult to establish a dominant angle through footwork alone. The instant you step off to your opponent's side to achieve a dominant angle, he squares his hips in relation to yours to eliminate it. To prevent this from happening, it's sometimes best to distract your opponent from your footwork, which can be achieved with your first strike in your combination. Although you might not land your first strike as a result of your neutral angle of attack, it gives you a dominant angle for the next strike in your combination. If you throw every strike with the intention of setting up the one to follow, you're guaranteed to cause damage with your combinations.

It is also very important to pay attention to your opponent's stance before throwing combinations. Certain combinations are more effective when you and your opponent have the same foot forward, and others are more effective when you and your opponent have opposite feet forward. And still other combinations are effective in both situations, but your targets change. To help you understand this concept a little better, I have broken combinations into two sections—same-stance combos, and opposite-stance combos. With more and more fighters learning how to fight from both a southpaw and standard stance, it is important not to focus on only one section.

HIGH-LOW PRINCIPLE

If you've trained in any of the striking arts such as karate, boxing, or Muay Thai, then you should already be familiar with the high-low principle. It's a fairly simple concept—strike high to pull your opponent's focus up to his head, and then strike low. It can also be done in reverse—strike low to force your opponent's focus onto his legs, and then go high with your next strike. The majority of combinations in this section follow this principle, and it is an important concept to grasp when putting together combinations of your own.

FEINTS

A feint is a fake strike, and the reason for throwing one should be either to blind your opponent or to generate a specific reaction that creates an opening for your next strike. In this section, I provide my favorite feinting techniques, but it is important for you to experiment and discover which feints work best for you. It is important to note that each feint is not designed for one specific strike. For example, in the first move of this subsection I show how to throw a blinding hand feint and then follow up with a reverse back elbow. Although the reverse back elbow is a strong technique to throw off the blinding hand, you could just as well substitute it for a punch, kick, or knee.

STRIKING TO THE CLINCH

To be a successful mixed martial artist, you must learn how to fight in all ranges of combat. As a result, in this section I demonstrate combinations that allow you to strike your way in and out of close range. I introduce the collar tie and reverse collar tie, and it is important to pay close attention to how I use these grips to off-balance my opponent and add power to my strikes. The focus of this subsection is not on the dozens of techniques you can utilize once you establish the clinch—that will be the focus of my next manual—but rather on how to strike your way into the clinch, cause some damage, and then strike your way back out.

SWITCH STEP STRAIGHT ATTACK

When you throw a straight punch at your opponent's centerline, the majority of the time he will react by backing away from you. If you remain planted firmly on both feet, your opponent will move out of punching range and escape your assault, which allows him to either recover from your first shot or plan his attack. However, if you step your rear foot forward as your opponent steps his lead foot back, you remain in punching range and can follow up with more strikes. With this technique, the goal is to land your second strike while your opponent is still shifting his stance to knock him off balance and create openings for even more strikes. This is what I demonstrate in the sequence below. I begin by landing a stiff jab to my opponent's chin. Momentarily blinded and fearing I will follow up with another strike, he steps his lead foot behind him and shifts from a southpaw stance into a standard stance. While he is still trying to reestablish his base in his new stance, I step my rear foot forward, putting me in a standard stance, and throw another stiff jab at his face. It's quite possible to chase your opponent across the ring in this manner. A prefect example is when Vitor Belfort fought Wanderlei Silva in UFC Brazil in 1998. Belfort hit Silva with a few good shots, forcing him to step backward. Instead of giving Silva space, Belfort continued to press forward with straight punches. In a matter of seconds, Belfort had punched Silva clear across the Octagon and knocked him out cold. In that particular situation, Belfort's continuous linear attack paid off, but I would not suggest training for this type of assault. Just as a linear retreat can get you into trouble, so can a long-winded linear attack. After all, every time you throw a straight punch, your opponent has options other than backward retreat. He can hold his ground and counter, zone to the side and evade your attack, or rush forward in an attempt to stifle your punches. If you get locked into linear mode past this initial one-two combination, your opponent can use it to his advantage. Later in the book I'll discuss how to deal with the other reactions your opponent can have to straight punches, but I included this one first because it is the most basic. It's an excellent way to capitalize on the primal instinct humans have to retreat linearly from a sudden head-on attack.

Feijao and I are in southpaw fighting stances, searching for an opening to attack.

I throw a jab at Feijao's chin.

3

Having landed the jab, Feijao attempts to retreat by stepping his lead foot behind him.

4

As Feijao backpedals, I pull my right hand back into my stance and step my rear foot forward to remain in striking range.

5

Planting my left foot in front of me and assuming a standard fighting stance, I rotate my hips and shoulders in a clockwise direction and throw a left jab at Feijao's chin.

BACK STEP PUNCHES

As I mentioned in the previous introduction, your opponent has four options when you attack his centerline with a straight punch. He can retreat backward, hold his ground and counter, zone to one side or the other, or rush forward. While your opponent's most common reaction will be to retreat, he is almost as likely to rush forward. In today's MMA, a lot of fighters will employ the good old-fashioned "bum rush" when they find themselves in a sticky situation. Their goal is to neutralize your attack by closing the distance and either landing a powerful punch such as an overhand, tying you up in the clinch, or securing a double-leg takedown without adequately setting it up. If you are unprepared to deal with your opponent charging forward, he's likely to accomplish his goal. To prevent such an outcome, in the sequence below I demonstrate how to step back and throw straight punches at the same time. When I fought Chris Leben in the UFC, I used this exact technique as he rushed toward me with a series of punches. Instead of trying to hold my ground and dodge his strikes, I stepped back and threw punches. With all his momentum moving forward, my strikes landed considerably harder than they would have if he had remained stationary.

To be most effective with this technique, it is important to coordinate your footwork with your strikes. If you step your right foot back, then you want to throw a straight strike with your right hand. If you step your left foot back, throw a straight strike with your left hand. When your timing is right, you'll usually stop your opponent's forward momentum dead. However, if he should continue to rush forward, you don't want to begin backpedaling in rapid succession because it will allow your opponent to catch up to your movement and land strikes of his own. In such a situation, you might want to back step a couple of times and then cut an angle off to the side to establish an even more dominant angle of attack. I strongly suggest spending a healthy amount of time developing this technique. Much of my success in MMA has to do with my ability to strike from every position and while moving in any direction. Becoming proficient at striking while backing up allows you to be both offensive and defensive at the same time, and that makes you a dangerous fighter indeed.

1) I've assumed a southpaw fighting stance.
2) I throw a jab at my imaginary opponent.
3) As I land the jab, my imaginary opponent rushes forward to close the distance. To prevent him from tying me up in the clinch, I step my lead foot back, assuming a standard fighting stance. 4) My imaginary opponent continues to come forward. To maintain distance, I step my left foot behind my right, returning to a southpaw stance. At the same time, I throw a left cross.

Feijao and are standing within punching range. We're both in southpaw fighting stances, searching for an opening to attack.

I throw a right jab at Feijao's chin.

In an attempt to tie me up in the clinch and avoid my second strike, Feijao steps his rear foot forward and assumes a standard fighting stance. To maintain distance, I step my right foot behind my left, also assuming a standard fighting stance.

Determined to establish the clinch, Feijao steps his right foot in front of his left, returning to a southpaw stance. To use his aggression against him, I step my left foot behind my right and throw a left cross to his chin.

JAB TO REAR HOOK

The jab to rear hook is a basic but very effective two-punch combination. To begin, throw a stiff jab into your opponent's face. As soon as your punch lands, step your rear foot to the outside of your opponent's lead leg to acquire a dominant angle of attack. Next, pull your lead hand back into your stance and fire off a hook with your rear arm. The key to being effective with this technique is throwing the jab with the intent of doing damage. A common mistake is to throw a weak jab and then step to the side to throw a powerful hook. If you don't threaten or rattle your opponent with the jab, he'll most likely see the hook coming and counter with an attack of his own. It's also very important that you blend the first punch, the side step, and the second punch together into one fluid movement. When done correctly, your opponent won't see the hook coming.

Feijao and I are in standard fighting stances, looking for an opening to attack.

I throw a left jab at Feijao's chin.

As I land the jab, I take a diagonal step forward with my right foot and place it to the outside of Feijao's lead leg. This gives me a dominant angle of attack.

I pull my left hand back into my stance and rotate my body in a counterclockwise direction.

Pivoting on the ball of my right foot, I rotate my hips and shoulders in a counterclockwise direction and throw a right hook toward Feijao's jaw.

Continuing to rotate my hips in a counterclockwise direction, I land a right hook to Feijao's jaw. Notice how I have kept my left arm elevated and shrugged my right shoulder to protect my face.

JAB / LEAD HOOK / REAR UPPERCUT

When you utilize the jab to lead hook to rear uppercut, you strike your opponent from odd angles, making it a very difficult combination for him to block or evade. If you look at the photos in the sequence below, you'll notice that I execute an outside slip immediately after throwing the jab to generate power for the hook. When done correctly, the movements involved in the slip makes it look as through you're preparing to follow the jab with a traditional right cross. As your opponent moves to defend against the cross, you land a powerful lead hook to his jaw. If the hook doesn't drop your opponent to the canvas, you will usually be in a good position to send a rear uppercut up between his arms and into his chin.

I'm squared off with Fred. Both of us are in standard fighting stances.

I throw a left jab at Feijao's chin.

I pull my left arm back into my stance, rotate my body in a counterclockwise direction, and come up onto the ball of my right foot.

Continuing to rotate my body in a counterclockwise direction, I elevate my right arm to protect my face and lower my left arm in preparation for my upcoming punch.

Whipping my hips in a clockwise direction, I pull my right shoulder back and throw a left hook toward the side of Feijao's jaw.

Still rotating my hips in a clockwise direction and pulling my right shoulder back, I land a powerful hook to Feijao's jaw.

I pull my left hand back into my stance, rotate my hips and shoulders in a counterclockwise direction, and throw a right uppercut toward Feijao's chin.

I land a right uppercut to Feijao's chin. Notice how I protect my face by keeping my left arm elevated and shrugging my right shoulder.

JAB TO OUTSIDE LOW KICK

The jab to outside low kick is a classic one-two combination that works on just about every opponent, regardless of his skill level. By throwing a stiff jab into your opponent's face, you force him to protect his head, which in turn pulls his focus away from his lower extremities. To follow up with the kick to the outside of his lead leg, pull your jab-hand back into your stance and use that momentum to help whip your hips circularly. The goal is to wind your hips up in one direction with the jab, and then unwind them in the opposite direction when you throw the kick. For the best results, there should be no delay between the two strikes. Another key ingredient to having success with this technique is throwing a powerful jab. If you fail to threaten your opponent with the jab, his focus won't shift upward, making it much more difficult to land the kick clean.

Feijao and I are in southpaw stances, searching for an opening to attack.

I take a small step forward with my right foot and land a jab to Feijao's chin.

I pull my right arm back into my stance, come up onto the ball of my left foot, and rotate my body in a clockwise direction.

Elevating my left arm to protect my head, I straighten my posture and distribute the majority of my weight onto my right leg.

Whipping my hips in a clockwise direction, I pull my right shoulder back and throw a left low kick toward the outside of Feijao's lead leg.

Still rotating my body in a clockwise direction, I pivot on the ball of my right foot, lean back to maintain my balance, throw my left arm to my side to further counterbalance my weight and generate power for my strike, and land a left low kick to the outside of Feijao's right leg. Notice how I have elevated my right arm to protect my head.

JAB / CROSS / OUTSIDE LOW KICK

In this sequence I demonstrate the jab to cross to outside low kick. It's similar to the previous combination in that you use your punches to pull your opponent's focus away from his legs, but the mechanics of the move are quite different. If you look at the photos below, you'll notice that I lead with a right jab. This spring-loads my hips to throw an attack from my left side. Instead of throwing a left kick as I did in the last sequence, I throw a left cross. This in turn spring-loads my hips for a right-sided attack. However, instead of utilizing my spring-loaded hips to throw a right kick, I follow the left cross with a left kick to the outside of my opponent's lead leg. The downside of throwing two strikes from the same side of your body at essentially the same time is that neither strike packs as much power. The upside is that your opponent has to protect both his upper and lower body at once, which is very difficult to manage. At first throwing two consecutive strikes from the same side of your body might seem awkward and unorthodox, but with practice and repetition, the combination should feel natural in no time. However, it is important to mention that the cross and low kick don't have to be thrown back-to-back. If your goal is to land the hardest kick possible, throw the cross, pull your arm back into your stance, reset your base, and then throw the low kick. I demonstrate this technique in the next sequence with a head kick.

Feijao and I are squared off in southpaw stances, hunting for an opening to attack.

I throw a right jab to Feijao's chin.

Pulling my right arm back into my stance, I come up onto the ball of my left foot, rotate my hips and shoulders in a clockwise direction, and throw a left cross toward Feijao's face.

Continuing to rotate my hips in a clockwise direction, I slightly drop my elevation and land a left cross to Feijao's chin.

Before Feijao can recover from the left cross, I pull my left arm back to protect my head, transfer the majority of my weight onto my right leg, and throw my right arm down to my side to maintain my balance and generate power for the coming kick.

Still rotating my hips in a clockwise direction, I lean slightly back to maintain my balance, pivot on my right foot, throw my right arm down to my side to further counterbalance my weight and generate power for my strike, and land a rear low kick to the outside of Feijao's lead leg.

JAB / CROSS / HEAD KICK

There are two differences between this combination and the previous one. The first difference has to do with timing. Instead of throwing the cross and then immediately following with the kick, I pull my cross hand back into my stance, reestablish my base, and then throw the kick. Although this doesn't allow me to overwhelm my opponent with two simultaneous strikes, it allows me generate a lot more power in my final blow. The second difference is that instead of targeting the outside of my opponent's lead leg with my kick, I target his head. Throwing the right cross and right head kick back-to-back is certainly an option, but in this particular case my goal is to land a kick so powerful that it blasts straight through my opponent's elevated arm and into the side of his head.

Feijao and I are in standard stances, searching for an opening to attack.

I throw a left jab at Feijao's chin.

3

I pull my left arm back into my stance, rotate my hips and shoulders in a counterclockwise direction, and throw a straight cross to Feijao's chin.

4

I pull my right arm back into my stance and reset my base.

5

Before Feijao can recover from the right cross, I come up onto the ball of my rear foot, distribute a larger portion of my weight onto my lead leg, and rotate my body in a counterclockwise direction.

6

I pull my left shoulder back, whip my hips in a counterclockwise direction, toss my right arm behind me to counterbalance my weight and generate power for my strike, and throw a right high kick to Feijao's head. Notice how I have elevated my left arm to protect my face.

JAB / LEAD FRONT KICK / JAB

If you're fighting an opponent who is shorter than you, he must work inside your range in order to land strikes. A good strategy against such an opponent is to use combinations such as the one demonstrated below to prevent him from closing the distance. Although the jab to lead straight front kick to jab probably won't produce a highlight-reel knockout, it is guaranteed to frustrate your opponent, which will often open up other attacking options. This particular combination also comes in handy when your opponent constantly advances forward. If you land each strike with power, he will think twice about blindly rushing into striking range. To use this combination effectively, begin by throwing a straight jab at your opponent's face. As you draw your lead hand back toward your body, lift your lead knee toward your chest to generate power for the kick. Once your knee is up, drive the ball of your foot into your opponent's abdomen. If you land a strong front kick, the force of the blow will cause your opponent to bend forward at the waist. Before he can straighten his body and reestablish his fighting stance, sneak a second jab between his guard.

Feijao and I are in standard fighting stances, looking for an opening to attack.

I throw a left jab at Feijao's chin.

Shifting my weight onto my right leg, I bend my knee and elevate my left foot straight off the mat to generate power for my coming kick.

Thrusting my hips forward, I throw a left front kick to Feijao's midsection. Notice how I lean back slightly to counterbalance my weight, as well as strike my target using the ball of my foot.

I retract my left leg, drop my foot straight to the mat, and reestablish my standard fighting stance.

The instant my left foot touches the mat, I throw a left jab at Feijao's chin.

CROSS / STEP / LOW KICK / LOW KICK

The cross is rarely used as a lead-in attack. The majority of the time it is utilized as a secondary attack immediately after a jab or lead hook. The reason for this is simple—being a rear-handed strike, the cross has to travel a greater distance to reach its target, making it easier for your opponent to spot and counter. If you begin by momentarily blinding your opponent with a lead-hand strike, your chances of landing the cross increase significantly. However, if you're up against an opponent who seldom uses side-to-side movement to evade your attacks, beginning a combination with a cross is an excellent way to force him into a backward retreat, which in turn sets you up for kicks. If you look at the sequence below, you'll notice that after working into punching range, I throw a hard cross at my opponent's face. The power of the punch and my opponent's lack of side-to-side movement cause him to step back and reverse his stance. Immediately I step my rear foot forward to remain in striking range. With my opponent's mind now focused on my hands and protecting his face, I throw a low kick to the outside of his lead leg. In an attempt to avoid my next strike and reestablish his base, my opponent steps his lead foot behind him a second time. Again I step my rear foot forward and throw a low kick to the outside of his lead leg. What makes this combination so effective is not just the fact that you're forcing your opponent to backpedal with a powerful cross, but you're also utilizing the high-low principle and attacking from multiple angles.

Feijao and I are in standard fighting stances, looking for an opening to attack.

I throw a right cross at Feijao's chin.

Having gotten hit with a stiff cross, Feijao attempts to create distance by stepping his left foot behind him. Instead of drawing my right arm back into my stance, I keep it extended and use the momentum of the punch to step my right foot forward into a southpaw stance. To capitalize on Feijao's stunned state, I need to follow up with a secondary strike as quickly as possible.

Pulling my right arm back into my stance, I come up onto the ball of my left foot, rotate my hips and shoulders in a clockwise direction, and shift my weight onto my right leg.

Whipping my hips in a clockwise direction, I pull my right shoulder back, throw my left arm behind me to maintain my balance and generate power for the strike, lean back slightly, and land a low kick to the outside of Feijao's right leg.

Immediately after I land the kick, Feijao again attempts to create distance by stepping his right leg behind him, returning to a standard stance. Instead of pulling my left leg back into my stance, I drop my foot straight down to the mat to remain in striking range.

The instant my left foot touches down on the mat, I come up onto the ball of my right foot, shift the majority of my weight onto my left leg, and rotate my body in a counterclockwise direction.

Whipping my hips in a counterclockwise direction, I pull my left shoulder back, throw my right arm behind me to counterbalance my weight and generate power for the kick, lean back slightly, and land a right low kick to the outside of Feijao's left leg. Notice how I protect my head by keeping my left arm elevated.

JAB TO REAR HOOK

In the previous section, I demonstrated how to execute a jab to rear hook combination when both you and your opponent are squared off in standard fighting stances. This is accomplished by throwing a left jab to his face, stepping your rear foot to the outside of his lead leg to acquire a dominant angle of attack, and then throwing a right hook to his jaw. Below I demonstrate the same combination, except now you and your opponent are in opposite fighting stances. The primary difference is how you acquire a dominant angle of attack. Instead of throwing the jab and then stepping your rear foot to the outside of your opponent's lead leg, you step your lead foot to the outside of your opponent's lead leg prior to throwing the jab. When you set the combination up in this fashion, there is no need for footwork after throwing the jab—you have already acquired a dominant angle of attack, and therefore can immediately transition into the rear hook.

Feijao is in a standard fighting stance, and I'm in a southpaw stance. Both of us are looking for an opening to attack. Notice how I have positioned my lead foot to the outside of his lead foot, giving me a dominant angle of attack.

I throw a right jab to Feijao's chin.

As I pull my right arm back into my stance, I begin rotating my hips and shoulders in a clockwise direction.

Keeping my right arm elevated to protect my face, I come up onto the ball of my left foot and throw a left hook toward Feijao's chin.

Continuing to rotate my hips in a clockwise direction, I pull my right shoulder back and land a left hook to Feijao's jaw. It is important to notice that my left hand, elbow, and shoulder are all aligned on the same horizontal plain. It is also important to notice that I am protecting my face by shrugging my left shoulder above my jaw and keeping my right arm elevated.

OPPOSITE STANCE

CROSS TO BODY / UPPERCUT ELBOW

In this sequence, I demonstrate how to throw a cross to your opponent's midsection and then follow up with a lead uppercut elbow to his head. If you look at the photos, you'll notice that I target my opponent's solar plexus with the cross rather than his face. I do this not only to knock the wind out of my opponent, but also to cause his head to lurch forward. Before he can pull his head back and reestablish his fighting stance, I drive a powerful uppercut elbow into his face. When practicing this technique, it is important to acquire a dominant angle of attack by stepping your lead foot to the outside of your opponent's lead leg as you throw the cross. It is also important to maintain your balance by slightly widening your base and dropping your level by bending at the knees. If you lean forward to land the cross, which is a common mistake, you'll lose the power generated from your legs and hips and your punch won't pack nearly as much sting. You also won't be in a good position to follow up with the uppercut elbow. To ensure you don't overextend your body when throwing the cross, keep your upper body centered and your weight evenly distributed on both legs.

Feijao is in a standard stance, and I'm in a southpaw stance. Both of us are looking for an opening to attack.

I take a diagonal step forward with my right foot, planting it to the outside of Feijao's lead leg, and assume a low stance by bending slightly at the knees.

I rotate my hips and shoulders in a clockwise direction, come up onto the ball of my left foot, and throw a left cross toward Feijao's midsection.

Still rotating in a clockwise direction, I land a left cross to Feijao's abdomen.

Shifting the majority of my weight onto my right leg, I slide my left foot forward and rotate my body in a counterclockwise direction.

Still rotating in a counterclockwise direction, I deliver a right uppercut elbow to the side of Feijao's head. It is important to notice that prior to throwing the cross, I obtained a dominant angle of attack by stepping my lead foot to the outside of Feijao's lead foot. This not only allowed me to land the cross, but also to move off to his side and land the uppercut elbow.

JAB / SIDE STEP / OUTSIDE LOW KICK

In the last section, I demonstrated how to throw a jab to outside low kick combination when you and your opponent are in the same fighting stance. It is a fairly simple combination—pump a jab into your opponent's face, and then follow up with a rear low kick to the outside of his lead leg. No footwork necessary. In the sequence below, I demonstrate how to land the same combination when your opponent is standing in an opposite fighting stance. If you look at the photos below, you'll notice I begin exactly the same, by throwing a jab at my opponent's face. However, due to the positioning of our feet, I now follow up with a lead low kick to my opponent's lead leg. In order to generate power for the strike, I step my rear foot forward and to the side after landing the jab. Employing this step not only allows me to create space between my opponent and me, but it also allows me to generate power for the lead kick. The target remains the same—the outside of my opponent's lead leg—but the setup and kick are quite different. If you don't feel comfortable throwing two kicks in a row from the same side of your body, the other option is to throw the jab and follow up with a rear low kick to your opponent's rear leg. But with the amount of distance you have to cover in order to land such a kick, you make yourself vulnerable to both counterstrikes and takedowns.

1

Feijao is in a standard stance, and I'm in a southpaw stance. Both of us are looking for an opening to attack.

2

I throw a straight right jab at Feijao's chin.

As I land the jab, I take a diagonal step forward with my left foot. This step not only creates more distance between Feijao's body and mine, but it also primes my hips to throw a more powerful kick.

Shifting my weight onto my left leg, I pull my left shoulder back, throw my right arm behind me to maintain my balance and generate power for the kick, rotate my hips in a counterclockwise direction, and throw my right leg toward the outside of Feijao's lead leg.

Leaning back slightly to maintain my balance, I land a right low kick to Feijao's left thigh.

JAB / FRONT KICK / UPPERCUT ELBOW

When you attack your opponent, his most common reaction will be to back up. I've offered several combinations that can be used to capitalize on this reaction, and here I offer another one. The more combinations you have to deal with your opponent's linear retreat, the more prepared you will be. In this sequence, I begin by throwing a jab, which causes my opponent to step his lead foot behind him and switch his stance. As his foot plants on the mat, I immediately throw a rear front kick to his midsection. This will typically yield one of two results. If he has not yet reestablished his base, the kick will most likely send him flying across the ring or cage. If he manages to quickly reset his base, then the kick will most likely cause his head to lurch forward. In such a situation, your best offensive option is to drop your leg straight down to the mat instead of pulling it back into your original stance. This will place you within striking range and allow you to throw an uppercut elbow to his face. However, there can be no hesitation between the kick and the elbow. If you take your time, your opponent will pull his head back and either put up his guard or launch a counterattack.

Feijao is in a standard stance, and I'm in a southpaw stance. Both of us are looking for an opening to attack.

I throw a right jab at Feijao's face.

As I pull my right arm back into my stance, I come up onto the ball of my left foot, shift the majority of my weight onto my right leg, and rotate my hips and shoulders in a clockwise direction.

To generate power for a rear front kick, I draw my left knee toward my chest.

I drive my hips forward, lean back to maintain my balance, and strike Feijao's abdomen using the ball of my foot. The power of the strike, as well as the pain it inflicts, causes his head to lurch downward.

Instead of pulling my leg back into my original fighting stance, I drop it straight down toward the mat so that I can remain in striking range and take advantage of Feijao's vulnerable state.

As I plant my left foot on the mat, I rotate my body in a clockwise direction and throw a left uppercut elbow toward Feijao's face.

Pressing my weight forward, I pull my left hand in front of my face and drive the tip of my elbow into Feijao's nose.

JAB / CROSS / STEP / ELBOW / KICK

Although it is important to learn how to apply forward pressure when attacking your opponent, it is just as important to learn when to release that pressure and back off. A lot of novice strikers will charge their opponent with a long-winded attack, but after throwing just a couple of strikes, their opponent neutralizes their attack by tying them up in the clinch. To prevent such a scenario, you must obtain the ability to strike your way into the pocket, do damage with strikes at close range, and then strike your way out of the pocket before your opponent can create a tie-up situation or launch a counterattack. The trick is learning how to read your opponent's movements. If he is hurt, you may be able to land numerous shots inside the pocket without risking a tie-up. However, if he is still sharp, you have to read his movements before he makes them and back away with strikes that turn his whole body into a target. The combination demonstrated in the sequence below is a perfect example of how to move in and out of range while attacking your opponent's entire body. I begin by momentarily blinding my opponent with a jab, which lets me move into close range. Immediately I throw two hard elbows to cause some damage while inside the pocket. Before my opponent can counter or tie me up in the clinch, I strike my way out of the pocket using a low kick. If you practice this combination and others like it, eventually the lines that separate the various ranges of combat will fade away and you'll move fluidly between them as though they were one, striking as you go.

Feijao is in a standard stance, and I'm in a southpaw stance. Both of us are searching for an opening to attack.

I throw a straight right jab to Feijao's chin.

As I pull my right arm back into my stance, I come up onto the ball of my rear foot, pull my right shoulder back, and rotate my hips in a clockwise direction.

I throw a left cross at Feijao's chin.

As I land the left cross, I move into close range by stepping my left foot in front of my right.

Pulling my left arm back into my stance, I shift the majority of my weight onto my left leg, come up onto the ball of my right foot, rotate my hips in a counterclockwise direction, and flare my right elbow out to the side.

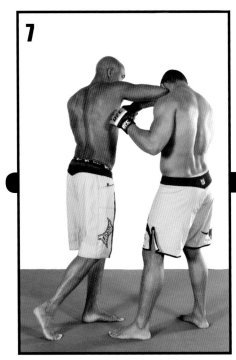

7 Pivoting on the ball of my right foot, I pull my left shoulder back, rotate my hips in a counterclockwise direction, and throw a right side-elbow to Feijao's jaw.

8 As I pull my right arm back into my stance, I reset my base and begin to throw my left elbow upward toward Feijao's chin.

9 Pulling my right shoulder back, I drive the tip of my left elbow upward into Feijao's chin.

10 Immediately after landing my left upward elbow, I place my left hand on Feijao's left shoulder.

11 I straighten my left arm and push Feijao backward.

12 Having created distance, I drop my left arm and throw a lead cut kick to the inside of Feijao's left thigh.

BLINDING HAND / REVERSE ELBOW

If you read the introduction to the basic reverse back elbow, then you already know that its is one of my favorite strikes. The instant I saw Tony Jaa employ this technique in the movie *Ong Bak*, I knew that it would work in mixed martial arts. However, I also knew that it wouldn't be the easiest strike to set up, especially on a game opponent. Against my trainers' better judgment, I began experimenting with various feints. I found several that were highly effective for setting up the reverse back elbow, but the blinding hand was at the top of the list. To execute this combination, extend your lead hand as if you were going to open-palm strike your opponent in the face. Your goal is not to land the strike, but rather obstruct his vision and cause him to flinch. As he reacts to the blinding hand, step forward into close range and throw a reverse back elbow upward between his arms and into his jaw. When done properly, your opponent won't know what hit him.

Feijao is in a standard stance, and I'm in a southpaw stance. Both of us are looking for an opportunity to attack.

I elevate my right arm and extend it toward Feijao's face.

As I extend my right arm, I open my hand and position my palm directly in front of Feijao's face. With this feint, I momentarily block his vision, generating a flinch reaction that distracts him from my coming strike.

Using the opening created by my feint to my advantage, I step my right foot forward and plant it to the inside of Feijao's left foot. As I close the distance between us, I drop my right arm, slightly turn my body in a counterclockwise direction, and chamber my right elbow by moving my right arm across my body. From here, I am in a perfect position to throw a reverse uppercut elbow to Feijao's chin.

Driving my hips and weight forward, I throw my right elbow upward between Feijao's guard and strike his chin.

SUPERMAN PUNCH / UPPERCUT ELBOW

Over the course of this book, I've demonstrated several combinations that follow the high-low principle, such as the jab to outside low kick. In this sequence I show the superman punch, a feinting technique that operates along the same lines. To execute this move, throw a fake rear low kick to draw your opponent's focus downward. The goal is to throw your leg far enough forward to get your opponent to react, but not so far that it jeopardizes your balance. If you bring your rear knee slightly past your lead leg, it's usually enough to sell your opponent on the kick. As your opponent prepares to defend against the kick, sprawl your kicking leg behind you, twist your hips, and throw a cross to his exposed face. In order to be effective with this technique, the fake kick and punch must be done in one fluid movement. If you stall between the two, your opponent will realize your intentions and possibly launch a counterattack. The best time to utilize the superman punch is after you've landed several hard low kicks. With your opponent's thigh already throbbing, he'll be more inclined to drop his guard when your rear knee comes forward. If you manage to land the cross clean, your opponent's world will undoubtedly be turned upside down. In this particular combination, I chose to follow up the cross by stepping my rear foot forward and throwing an upward elbow into my opponent's jaw.

Feijao is in a standard stance, and I'm in a southpaw stance. Both of us are looking for an opening to attack.

I fake a rear kick by bringing my left knee forward. At the same time, I cock my left arm back and prepare to throw a cross. It is important to notice that I only bring my left knee slightly past my lead leg. If you exaggerate your movement, it will be hard to pull your leg back and throw the cross.

3

Jerking my left leg behind me, I rotate my hips in a clockwise direction throw a left cross at Feijao's face. Notice how as I shoot my leg back I rock my upper body forward to maintain my balance and generate more power for the punch.

4

Using the rocking motion of my body, I deliver a powerful left cross to Feijao's chin.

5

Due to the power behind my cross, Feijao gets knocked backward. To stay within striking range and capitalize on his stunned-state, I step my left foot in front of my right and assume a standard fighting stance. Notice how I keep my right arm up to protect my face and my left arm extended to gauge distance and keep Feijao off balance.

6

As I pull my left arm back into my stance, Feijao tilts his body forward to maintain his balance. Immediately I come up onto the ball of my right foot, rotate my hips in a counterclockwise direction, pull my left shoulder back, and throw a right uppercut elbow into his chin.

FAKE SUPERMAN PUNCH / HOOK / ELBOW

The superman punch is an excellent feinting technique, but it is utilized by a vast majority of MMA competitors. As a result, it is becoming an increasingly more difficult technique to pull off, especially when up against a fighter familiar with the movements. If you attempt a superman punch and your opponent defends against it, a good option is to employ the technique as a feint. In the sequence below, I bring my rear leg forward to fake a kick, but instead of sprawling my kicking leg back and throwing a superman punch, I step my rear foot forward and switch my stance. This puts me into close range with my opponent, and I immediately throw a rear hook followed by a lead uppercut.

Feijao is in a standard stance, and I'm in a southpaw stance. Both of us are looking for an opening to attack.

I fake a superman punch by throwing my rear leg forward and cocking my left arm back.

Instead of sprawling my left leg back and throwing a left cross at Feijao's face, I step my left foot to the inside of his left foot, shift my weight onto my left leg, rotate my hips and shoulders in a counterclockwise direction, and throw a right hook to his jaw.

Having caught Feijao off guard by faking the superman punch and then throwing a right hook, I immediately move on to my secondary attack by pulling my right shoulder back, rotating my hips in a clockwise direction, and throwing a left uppercut elbow between his guard and up toward his chin.

Continuing to rotate my hips and shoulders in a clockwise direction, I drive the tip of my left elbow into Feijao's chin.

FEINTS

FEINT HEAD MOVEMENT / HOOK / UPPERCUT

Head movement is an excellent way to create openings and set up attacks. Two perfect examples are the inside and outside slip. When you execute an inside slip, your movements are similar to the beginning movements of a jab, and when you execute an outside slip, your movements are similar to the beginning movements of a cross. More often than not, your opponent will react to your head movement instead of waiting for you to throw the following strike. As his guard shifts to defend either the jab or cross, you have a perfect opening to throw an alternate strike such as a lead hook. In addition to disguising your attack, slipping your head from side to side also makes it harder for your opponent to zero in on your head and land clean strikes. In the sequence below, I execute an inside to outside slip to throw off my opponent's defenses. As I slip my head to the outside, I take advantage of his distracted state by throwing a powerful lead hook to his face and then following up with a rear uppercut.

Feijao is in a standard stance, and I'm in a southpaw stance. Both of us are looking for an opening to attack.

I execute an inside slip by rotating my hips and shoulders in a counterclockwise direction, sinking my hips back slightly, and dipping my head toward my left side. My goal with executing this movement and the one to come next is to disguise my attack and close the distance between Feijao and me.

I execute an outside slip by rotating my hips and shoulders in a clockwise direction, dipping my head toward my right side, and coming up onto the ball of my left foot. With my upper body now on Feijao's left side, I am in a perfect position to acquire a dominant angle of attack and throw a powerful right hook to his jaw.

I step my right foot to the outside of Feijao's left foot to acquire a dominant angle of attack. In one fluid motion, I rotate my hips in a counterclockwise direction, pivot on my right foot, pull my left shoulder back, and land a right hook to Feijao's jaw. In order not to stifle the momentum generated by my rotating hips, I allow my left foot to slide circularly behind my right leg.

Pulling my right arm back into my stance, I rotate my hips in a clockwise direction, pull my right shoulder back, and throw a left uppercut between Feijao's guard and up toward his chin.

I land a powerful rear uppercut to Feijao's chin.

JAB TO MUAY THAI CLINCH

In this sequence, I demonstrate how to secure the Muay Thai clinch when your opponent backs away from an attack. If you look at the photos below, you'll notice that as I establish the clinch my opponent continues to backpedal. To compensate for his retreat, I step forward, putting me in range to drive a straight knee into his midsection.

Feijao is in a standard stance, and I'm in a southpaw stance. Both of us are looking for an opening to attack.

I throw a right jab to Feijao's jaw.

After getting hit with my jab, Feijao steps his left foot behind him in an attempt to avoid my secondary strike. To stay within striking range and capitalize on his stunned-state, I step my left foot forward and assume a standard fighting stance.

Rotating my hips and shoulders in a clockwise direction, I pull my right arm back into my stance and wrap my left hand around the back of Feijao's head.

Rotating my body in a counterclockwise direction, I punch my right arm past the left side of Feijao's head and then wrap my right hand over my left hand.

I step my right foot in front of my left.

In an attempt to escape my control, Feijao steps his right foot backward. Before he can mount a defense, I step my left foot forward to stay in close range and use my arms to pull his head down into my right shoulder. This last step is very important because it not only allows you to drive in a more powerful strike, but it also protects you from counterstrikes such as uppercuts and hooks.

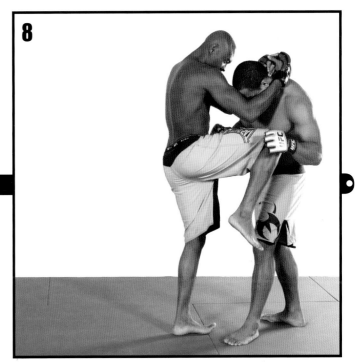

Keeping Feijao's head pinned to my right arm, I drive a powerful straight knee into his midsection using my right leg.

CROSS / STEP / HOOK / KNEE

When you're in the same fighting stance as your opponent, stepping your rear foot to the outside of his lead leg gives you a dominant angle from which to attack, and when you're in an opposite fighting stance, stepping your lead foot to the outside of his lead leg provides you with a dominant angle from which to attack. Over the course of this book, I've offered numerous striking combinations that show how this dominant angle can be utilized. In this sequence, I take it one step further by demonstrating how to use a dominant angle to establish the clinch and deliver a powerful knee strike. The technique is set up the same as the others—attack your opponent's centerline with a straight strike, and then step to the outside of his lead leg to acquire a dominant angle of attack. In this particular sequence, I opt to begin my attack with a right cross. Once I've shifted the positioning of my feet, I follow up with a left hook to my opponent's jaw. With my opponent stunned from my first two strikes, I secure a reverse collar tie by wrapping my left hand around the left side of his head, force his head down, and throw a straight knee to his abdomen. The nice part about the reverse collar tie is that it allows you to maintain distance, protect yourself from counterattacks, and add power to the knee strike by driving your opponent's head downward. It is important to note that in this situation, you have the option of delivering either a straight or side knee. To see how the side knee can be utilized in a similar scenario, flip to the next technique.

Feijao and I are in standard stances, searching for an opening to attack.

I land a right cross to Feijao's chin.

As I pull my right arm back into my stance, I take a diagonal step forward with my right foot, planting it to the outside of Feijao's left leg to acquire a dominant angle of attack.

Distributing a larger portion of my weight onto my right leg, I come up onto the ball of my left foot, pull my right shoulder back, rotate my hips in a clockwise direction, and throw a vicious left hook between Feijao's guard and into his chin.

Instead of pulling my left arm back into my stance, I circle it around the left side of Feijao's head and wrap my hand around the back of his neck.

I drive my right knee upward into Feijao's midsection.

FRONT KICK / CROSS / SWITCH STEP / KNEE

This combination is very similar to the previous one in that I attack my opponent's centerline with straight strikes, step to the outside of his lead leg to close the distance and acquire a dominant angle of attack, tie him up with a reverse collar tie, and then deliver a powerful knee to his midsection. The primary difference is with the strikes that I throw. In this sequence, I begin with a front kick to my opponent's midsection and then follow it with a cross. Next, I step to the outside of his body, secure the clinch, and throw a side knee to his solar plexus. Both combinations are equally effective—deciding which one to utilize boils down to personal preference and the situation you're presented with. If you're up against an opponent who constantly presses forward, beginning the combination with a front kick is a good way to maintain distance. If your opponent is a master at defending against kicks, you may want to utilize the previous combination and begin with a cross.

Feijao and I are in standard stances, searching for an opening to attack.

Shifting my weight onto my rear leg, I lift my left foot off the mat and prepare to throw a lead front kick.

I lift my left knee toward my chest, and then thrust my hips forward and strike Feijao's abdomen using the ball of my foot.

I drop my left foot straight down to the mat and reestablish a standard stance.

The instant I plant my left foot on the mat, I rotate my hips in a counterclockwise direction, shift my weight to my lead leg, pivot on the ball of my right foot, pull my left shoulder back, and throw a right cross to Feijao's chin.

Elevating my left arm for protection, I pull my right arm back into my stance, step my right foot to the outside of Feijao's left leg to assume a southpaw stance and acquire a dominant angle of attack, and shift my weight onto my right leg.

I reach my left arm past the left side of Feijao's head, rotate my hips in a clockwise direction, dip my right shoulder toward my right side, and throw my left knee toward Feijao's midsection.

I place my left hand on Feijao's left shoulder and I drive my knee into his solar plexus.

JAB / STEP / ELBOW / CLINCH COMBO

When you string together a combination of strikes, each technique should create an opening for the following technique. The combination below is a perfect example. I begin by throwing a right jab to my opponent's face, which momentarily blinds him and allows me to land a reverse back elbow. The reverse back elbow forces his head upward, which exposes his face and creates an opening for me to land a right side-elbow. If you look at the photos closely, you'll notice that I push my opponent's head away from me using my left hand as I land the right side-elbow, creating enough space for me to maneuver my right elbow toward the center of his chest and secure a right collar tie. The instant I secure the collar tie, my opponent defensively pushes back into me, but I use his momentum against him by wrapping my left arm around his head and securing the Muay Thai clinch. Once I have secured this dominant position, I pull his head down and drive my knee upward into his face. If you can put your combinations together so that each strike sets up the next, you'll not only land a larger percentage of the time, but you'll also make it very difficult for your opponent to defend or counter with an attack of his own.

Feijao is in a standard stance, and I'm in a southpaw stance. Both of us are looking for an opening to attack.

I land a right jab to Feijao's chin.

Pulling my right arm back into my stance, I rotate my hips and shoulders in a clockwise direction and come up onto the ball of my rear foot.

Continuing to rotate my hips and shoulders in a clockwise direction, I move into close range by stepping my left foot in front of my right.

The instant my left foot touches down, I twist my body in a clockwise direction, come up onto the ball of my left foot, drop my elevation by bending at the knees, and slide my left arm across my body toward my right side to generate power for the reverse back elbow.

Driving forward and upward off my right leg, I snap my hips in a counterclockwise direction and throw my left elbow upward between Feijao's guard, connecting solidly with his chin using the point of my elbow.

Using the momentum generated by the reverse back elbow, I rotate my hips and shoulders in a counterclockwise direction, pull my left arm back into my stance, come up onto the ball of my right foot, and throw a side elbow along a circular path toward the left side of Feijao's jaw.

Shifting a larger portion of my weight onto my left leg, I continue to rotate my hips in a counterclockwise direction and pull my left shoulder back. Having elevated Feijao's head with my reverse back elbow strike, I land a clean side elbow to his jaw.

The instant I land the side elbow, I place my left hand on the left side of Feijao's head.

I push Feijao's head away from me using my left hand. This creates the distance I need to move my right elbow toward the center of his chest.

I wrap my right hand around the back of Feijao's head and curl my right elbow toward the center of his chest to form a right collar tie. At the same time, I release the pressure I was applying with my left hand and circle my left arm around to the right side of his head.

No longer applying pressure to Feijao's head using my left hand, he turns into me to square our hips. Using his movement to my advantage, I wrap my left hand around the back of his head to secure the Muay Thai clinch, step my left foot back, drop my hips, and pull his head downward. Notice how my elbows are pinched tightly together to prevent him from pulling his head free.

Still pulling down on Feijao's head, I drive my left knee into his chin.

PUNCH COMBO / ELBOW / SIDE CLINCH

This combination is similar to others I've shown in that I punch my way into close range, use elbow strikes to open my opponent up, and then finish with a knee from the clinch. The primary difference is that I use a different set of strikes to close the distance, and once I get into close range, I secure the side-clinch instead of the Muay Thai clinch. If you look at the photos in the sequence below, you'll notice that I set up the side clinch by establishing a reverse collar tie on the right side of my opponent's head using my right hand. Next, I add leverage and control to the hold by gripping my right wrist with my left hand. With both of my arms now controlling my opponent's head, it is much easier to force his face downward into my rising knee strike. When you land this final blow clean, it's guaranteed to produce positive results.

Feijao is in a standard stance, and I'm in a southpaw stance. Both of us are searching for an opening to attack.

I land a right jab to Feijao's chin.

As I pull my right arm back into my stance, I rotate my hips and shoulders in a clockwise direction, come up onto the ball of my left foot, and throw a left cross to Feijao's chin.

Having taken two shots, Feijao attempts to avoid my next strike by stepping his left foot behind him and assuming a southpaw stance. To land my third strike in the combination, I immediately step my left foot forward, pull my left arm back into my stance, rotate my hips and shoulders in a counterclockwise direction, and throw a right uppercut toward his chin.

5

Continuing to rotate my hips and shoulders in a counterclockwise direction, I slide my right foot toward my left and throw a right uppercut between Feijao's guard and into his chin. Notice how the impact of the strike forces his head upward.

6

Pulling my right arm back into my stance, I rotate my hips in a clockwise direction, raise my elevation by straightening my left leg, shift my weight forward, and reach my left hand behind my head in preparation for the elbow strike.

7

Still rotating my body in a clockwise direction, I drive my left elbow downward into the right side of Feijao's jaw.

8

After landing the downward elbow, I drive my left forearm into the right side of Feijao's neck. Notice how this action creates distance between us and forces his head to turn toward his left side.

9

Maintaining space between Feijao and my body using my left arm, I slide my right arm across the right side of his face and wrap my right hand around the back of his head.

10

I force Feijao's head toward the mat using my right hand.

11

I grab the top of my right forearm with my left hand. This hold gives me more leverage to force Feijao's head downward.

12

Driving Feijao's head toward the mat using my arms, I throw my right knee upward into his face.

PUSH BLOCK / PUNCH-KICK-KNEE COMBO

In the sequence below, I attack my opponent with an aggressive combination of strikes and push blocks. Just as with the previous combination, each strike sets up the one to follow. If you look at the photos, you'll notice that I target my opponent's entire body and use multiple angles of attack. By striking and off-balancing him in this manner, I keep him on the defensive, making it nearly impossible for him to block or counter with an attack of his own. It is important to note that the push blocks demonstrated in this sequence are excellent tools for gauging and maintaining distance, especially against opponents who attempt to neutralize your attacks by coming forward.

Feijao is in a standard stance, and I'm in a southpaw stance. Both of us are looking for an opening to attack.

I land a right jab to Feijao's chin.

Instead of pulling my right arm back into my stance, I come up onto the ball of my left foot, drive my weight forward, and push my right hand into Feijao's chest. This push block accomplishes two things—it prevents Feijao from closing the distance and tying me up in the clinch, which would nullify my attack, and it forces his weight onto his rear leg, which disrupts his base and sets me up for my next strike.

Having off-balanced Feijao with my push block, I step my right foot to the outside of his left foot to acquire a dominant angle of attack, pull my right arm back into my stance, rotate my hips and shoulders in a clockwise direction, and throw a left hook between his guard and into his chin.

5

Instead of pulling my left arm back into my stance, I place my left hand on Feijao's left shoulder. By applying outward pressure with my hand and rotating my body in a counterclockwise direction, I not only set myself up to throw a powerful uppercut, but I also prevent Feijao from turning into me, which would eliminate my dominant angle of attack.

6

Pulling my left hand back into my stance, I rotate my hips and shoulders in a counterclockwise direction and throw a right uppercut between Feijao's arms and into his chin.

7

Pulling my right shoulder back and rotating my hips in a clockwise direction, I throw a left cross to Feijao's jaw.

8

Instead of pulling my left arm back into my stance, I secure a reverse collar tie by wrapping my left hand around the back of Feijao's head. I also shift the majority of my weight onto my right leg to set up a left low kick.

9

Pulling Feijao's head down using my left arm, I whip my hips in a clockwise direction and throw a left low kick to his right thigh.

10

Still forcing Feijao's head down using my left arm, I pull my left leg back into my stance, rotate my hips in a counterclockwise direction, and throw a right uppercut toward his chin.

11

I throw my right uppercut underneath Feijao's left arm and connect solidly to his chin.

12

I pull my right arm back and move it above my left arm.

I place my right hand over my left hand and then use my arms to drive Feijao's head toward the mat.

I slide my left foot forward.

Shifting my weight onto my left leg, I drive Feijao's head down and I throw my right knee upward into his face.

COUNTERATTACKS

One of the major goals in fighting is to make your opponent pay every time he attacks you. In this section, I demonstrate how to accomplish this by combining strikes with evasion, blocking, and checking techniques. When you're successful, you not only avoid your opponent's attack, but you also break his rhythm by hitting him with an attack of your own. For example, at the beginning of the section I offer several ways to counter your opponent's jab with a jab of your own. Just as his fist sails past the side of your head, your fist collides with his face. As long as your timing is correct, your opponent will have a very difficult time throwing a second strike due to his disrupted rhythm. This allows you to immediately follow your jab with another strike, and then another.

Just as with attacks, the counterattacks at your disposal will depend upon the stance you and your opponent are in. If you have the same foot forward, different counterattacks will be available than when you have the opposite foot forward. To help you down this road, I've broken the section into two subsections—same-stance counters and opposite-stance counters. With combinations in both, it is very important that you pay attention to how to acquire a dominant angle of attack.

At the end of this section, I demonstrate a number of techniques you can employ to counter your opponent's kicks. In addition to showing how to counter after checking a kick, I also demonstrate how to catch a kick and counter while holding on to his leg. Although checking is the safer of the two techniques, catching a kick creates a host of counterattacking opportunities.

COUNTER JAB WITH JAB

If you've spent some time practicing the techniques I've already demonstrated, you should be quite familiar with the jab. You understand how to throw a jab, and you understand how to evade your opponent's jab using either a slip or a parry. In the sequences below, I demonstrate how to blend jab offense and jab defense together. To accomplish this, all you have to do is evade your opponent's jab and throw a jab of your own at the same time. If you look at the photos, you'll notice that in each of the three techniques my jab lands just as my opponent's jab arm reaches the end of its extension. This is key because when you hit an opponent while he is in the middle of a strike, it disrupts his rhythm, which in turn creates openings for you to follow up with a secondary attack.

The first counter I demonstrate is called the lean back parry (Sequence A). To evade your opponent's jab in this technique, you lean your head back and catch his fist in the palm of your rear hand. At the same time, you throw a jab with your lead hand. Since this technique involves no side-to-side head movement, it is best utilized on opponents who have an inferior reach. The second counter I offer is a basic inside slip, which involves slipping your head away from your centerline while throwing a jab of your own at the same time (Sequence B). The third counter I show is the parry slip, which is essentially a combination of the first two methods (Sequence C). To execute this technique, simultaneously parry your opponent's jab using your rear hand, execute an inside slip, and throw a jab straight down the pipe. I suggest drilling all three techniques relentlessly. Remember, your goal is to break your opponent's rhythm by slipping his punch and landing a jab at the same time. If successful, a plethora of secondary attacks will be made available, many of which I will demonstrate over the course of this section.

(A) Lean Back Counter

Feijao and I are in southpaw stances, searching for an opening to attack.

Feijao throws a jab at my face. To counter, I lean back slightly, open my left hand, and throw a jab at his face.

With my face no longer in range of Feijao's jab, I catch his fist in the palm of my left hand. At the exact moment that his punch reaches the end of its extension, my jab lands to his face. It is important to mention that this technique should be reserved for when you're fighting an opponent with a shorter reach.

(B) Slip Counter

1) Feijao and I are in southpaw stances, searching for an opening to attack.

2) Feijao throws a right jab at my face. To counter, I slip my head toward my left side and throw a right jab at his face.

3) By slipping my head away from my centerline, Feijao's fist sails past my head. Just as his arm reaches the end of its extension, I land a stiff jab to his face.

SAME STANCE

(C) Parry Slip Counter

Feijao and I are in standard stances, searching for an opening to attack.

Feijao throws a left jab at my face. To counter, I parry his left hand toward my left side using my right hand, slip my head toward my right side, and throw a left jab toward his face.

By slipping my head away from my centerline and redirecting Feijao's punch toward my left side, his fist sails past my head. Just as his arm reaches the end of its extension, I land a stiff jab to his face.

COUNTER JAB WITH JAB / CROSS / HIGH KICK

As I mentioned in the previous sequence, when you counter an opponent's jab with a jab, you break his rhythm, creating an opportunity to follow up with a combination. In the sequence below, I follow the jab with a left cross, which is the most basic and natural secondary attack that can be implemented off this particular counter. To increase my chances of knocking my opponent out, I follow the left cross with a left kick to the head. It is important to note that after landing the cross, you can either throw the kick immediately or reset your base and then throw the kick. The former is the quickest, but the latter produces the most power. Deciding which option to chose boils down to personal preference and the situation at hand. In this particular sequence, I opt to immediately throw the kick rather than reset my base.

Feijao and I are in southpaw stances, searching for an opening to attack.

Feijao throws a right jab at my face. To slip and counter his punch, I drop my left shoulder, move my head toward my left side, and throw a right jab at his face. As his jab glides past my head, I land my jab.

Immediately after landing the jab, I pull my right arm back into my stance, come up onto the ball of my left foot, rotate my hips in a clockwise direction, and throw a left cross at Feijao's face.

Immediately after landing the left cross, I throw my left arm behind me, snap my hips in a clockwise direction, and throw a left round kick at Feijao's head.

COUNTER JAB WITH JAB / CROSS / MID KICK

In this sequence I begin my attacking combination with a jab and a cross just as I did in the last sequence, but instead of following up with a rear kick to the head, I throw a hard rear kick at my opponent's ribs. While this combination is heavily utilized in Muay Thai matches, it can be a little risky in MMA due to your opponent's ability to catch your kick and execute a takedown. To avoid such an outcome, I'll usually reserve mid-kicks for when I rattle my opponent, put him in a strictly defensive mode, or have him backpedaling.

Feijao and I are in southpaw stances, searching for an opening to attack.

Feijao throws a right jab at my face. To slip and counter his punch, I drop my left shoulder, move my head toward my left side, and throw a right jab at his face. Just as his punch sails past my head, I connect with his chin.

Pulling my right arm back into my stance, I come up onto the ball of my left foot and whip my hips in a clockwise direction.

Still rotating my hips in a clockwise direction, I land a left cross to Feijao's jaw.

Instead of pulling my left arm back into my stance, I shift the majority of my weight onto my right leg and prepare to unleash a left round kick.

Still whipping my hips in a clockwise direction, I pull my right shoulder back and throw a left round kick to Feijao's midsection, striking his liver with my shinbone.

SAME STANCE

COUNTER JAB WITH JAB / UPPERCUT / JAB

In this sequence, I counter my opponent's jab with a jab, step my rear foot to the outside of his lead leg to obtain a dominant angle of attack, and then throw a rear uppercut to his chin. The goal is twofold—land your jab just as your opponent's jab sails by the side of your head, and land the uppercut before he can pull his jab back into his stance. The former allows you to disrupt his rhythm, and the latter allows you to sneak your uppercut underneath his outstretched arm and connect solidly with his chin. If you don't knock your opponent out with the uppercut, he will most likely turn into you to square his hips with yours and eliminate your dominant angle. In such a scenario, a good option is to circle in the opposite direction of his turn and throw a second jab just as he comes around to face you. This last strike not only allows to you remain offensive, but it also prevents your opponent from coming forward with a potential counterattack.

1

Feijao and I are in southpaw stances, searching for an opening to attack.

2

Feijao throws a right jab at my face. To slip and counter his punch at the same time, I drop my left shoulder, move my head toward my left side, and throw a right jab at his face. Just as his fist slips past my head, I land my punch to his chin.

As I pull my right hand back into my stance, I step my left foot forward and to the outside of Feijao's right leg, giving me a dominant angle of attack. Notice how I have placed my left foot slightly in front of my right foot. This will allow me to rotate into a southpaw stance.

I rotate my hips in a clockwise direction, come up onto the ball of my left foot, pull my right shoulder back, and throw a left uppercut underneath Feijao's right arm and into his chin. Notice how my rotation has put me in a perfect southpaw stance.

In an attempt to eliminate my dominant angle of attack, Feijao turns to face me. Before he can accomplish his goal, I pull my left arm back into my stance, rotate my body in a counterclockwise direction, and pivot on my right foot until I have completed a forty-five-degree turn.

While Feijao is still turning to face me, I use my inside pivot to generate power and throw a right jab to Feijao's chin. It is important to note that I timed my jab to land just as Feijao turned to face me.

COUNTER JAB WITH JAB / REAR KNEE

In this sequence I counter my opponent's jab with a jab and then follow up with a straight knee to his midsection. It's a little different than some of the previous secondary attacks I've shown in that instead of throwing my counter jab, pulling my arm back into my stance, and then executing my follow-up strike, I throw the knee strike almost at the same time as the jab, which requires me to leave my jab extended as I launch my knee. The goal is to land the knee while your opponent's arm is still fully extended and his ribs are exposed. When you time it right, you're guaranteed to take the wind from your opponent's lungs, perhaps even shatter a couple of ribs. The best time to use this strike is when you're in close range with your opponent or when he leans his upper body forward in an attempt to generate more power with his jab.

Feijao and I are in standard fighting stances, searching for an opening to attack.

Feijao throws a left jab at my face. To counter, I parry his fist toward my left using my right hand, slip my head toward my right side, and throw a left counter jab at his face. Notice how I shift my weight onto my lead leg as I connect—this sets me up to throw a rear knee into Feijao's midsection.

While the momentum of Feijao's jab still carries him forward, I drive my right knee into his midsection. It is important to note that this technique works especially well against opponents who tend to lean into their jabs in an attempt to generate more power because it takes them longer to retract their arm.

COUNTER JAB WITH JAB / HIGH KNEE

There are currently a large number of wrestlers competing in MMA, and a sizable portion of those wrestlers employ similar tactics when advancing upon their opponent. Constantly on the hunt for a takedown, they assume a low stance and come toward you throwing a series of jabs. Sometimes their intent is to blind you with a jab and then shoot for a double- or single-leg takedown, and other times their goal is to bait you into throwing a counterstrike that they can duck under, giving them easy access to your legs. When faced with this type of opponent, countering his jab with a jab and then throwing a high knee is an excellent option. It's not an easy technique to time, but landing the knee strike clean is an excellent way to put your opponent to sleep. If you look at the photos below, you'll notice that my opponent maintains a high stance throughout the sequence and my knee strike falls short of his face. This is simply for safety purposes. When you're in a fight, you want to target either your opponent's midsection or chin.

Feijao and I are in southpaw stances, searching for an opening to attack.

Feijao throws a right jab at my face. To slip and counter his punch at the same time, I drop my left shoulder, move my head toward my left side, and throw a right jab at his chin.

Pulling my right arm back into my stance, I rotate my body in a clockwise direction, come up onto the ball of my left foot, and drive my left arm into the back of Feijao's right arm. The goal is to redirect his arm toward my right side, forcing his hips to turn in a counterclockwise direction, which in turn disrupts his base and balance.

Having forced Feijao's right arm toward my right side, it becomes more difficult for him to pull his arm back into his stance. While his right arm is still extended, I grab his right wrist with my right hand and drive my knee upward into his face.

COUNTER JAB WITH SPINNING BACK ELBOW

The spinning back elbow is an excellent technique to utilize in Muay Thai competition, but it's a little risky for MMA. The instant you expose your back, your opponent has a number of options at his disposal, such as securing a body-lock or executing a takedown. The majority of the time, the rewards just aren't worth the risks. However, it is still a good technique to have in your arsenal. If your opponent's clinch and takedowns are weak, or you have him wounded on his feet and want to finish him with a highlight reel knockout, the rewards go up and the risk goes down. In the sequence below, I demonstrate how to employ this beautiful attack as a counter to the straight jab.

Feijao and I are in southpaw stances, searching for an opening to attack.

Feijao throws a right jab at my face. To evade his punch, I parry his fist toward my right side using my left hand and slip my head toward my left side.

As Feijao's fist sails by the side of my head, I step my right foot to the outside of his lead leg. However, instead of planting my entire foot on the mat, I come down on the ball. This allows me to rotate my body in a counterclockwise direction with ease.

Still rotating my body in a counterclockwise direction, I drop my right heel to the mat and distribute a larger portion of my weight onto my right leg.

Continuing to rotate my body in a counterclockwise direction, I pivot on my right foot, slide my left foot toward Feijao's right foot, and throw my left elbow straight back into his chin.

COUNTER JAB / COUNTER HOOK

Sometimes countering your opponent's jab with one of your own isn't enough to thwart his attack. If he maintains his rhythm and manages to throw a secondary attack before you can launch your secondary attack, switch from an attacking mind-set to a counterattacking mind-set. The sequence below is a perfect example. I counter my opponent's jab with a jab, but before I can throw a follow-up strike, he comes forward with a rear hook. Instead of trying to beat him to the punch, which would be difficult in this situation because he already has the jump on me, I lean back, allowing his hook to sail by my face. Without letting him recover his stance, I immediately throw a counter lead hook and strike him square in the jaw. Having disrupted his rhythm with this last blow, I can switch back to an attacking mind-set and launch follow-up strikes.

Feijao and I are in southpaw stances, searching for an opening to attack.

Feijao throws a right jab at my face. To counter his punch, I drop my left shoulder, slip my head toward my left side, and throw a right jab at his jaw.

As I pull my lead arm back into my stance, Feijao throws a left hook toward the right side of my head.

To evade Feijao's left hook, I shift the majority of my weight onto my left leg and lean my head back. At the same time, I prepare to throw a right hook by dropping my right arm. It is important not to drop your arm unless you know you can lean back far enough to avoid your opponent's punch, yet not lose your balance. If you are in close range, a better option would be to bob and weave underneath the hook.

As Feijao's hook sails in front of my face, I counter with a lead right hook, hitting him in the side of jaw.

COUNTER JAB TO KNEE DESTRUCTION

This sequence is similar to the previous one in that I counter my opponent's jab with a jab, but fail to break his rhythm. Before I can throw my second strike, he launches a straight knee at my midsection. Instead of attempting to evade his strike, I throw a downward elbow into his knee. When you time the technique so that the downward momentum of your elbow meets the upward momentum of his knee, you'll cause a significant amount of damage and immediately take his leg out of the fight.

Feijao and I are in southpaw stances, searching for an opening to attack.

Feijao throws a right jab at my face. To counter his punch, I drop my left shoulder, dip my head toward my left side, and throw a right jab at his jaw.

As I pull my right arm back into my stance, Feijao steps his right foot forward and prepares to throw a rear knee.

Understanding Feijao's intentions by reading his body movement, I begin my counter by pulling my right arm back into my stance, coming up onto the ball of my left foot, and rotating my body in a clockwise direction.

As Feijao throws his left knee upward toward my midsection, I rotate my body in a clockwise direction, sink my weight toward the mat by bending at the knees, and driving a left downward elbow into his thigh. The downward momentum of my elbow coupled with the upward momentum of Feijao's knee produces a very powerful strike that has a devastating effect on the muscles and nerves of his leg.

LEAD ARM BLOCK TO CROSS COUNTER

I begin this sequence by deflecting my opponent's jab using a lead arm block. Instead of letting him pull his arm back into his stance, I immediately rotate my body and throw a cross. If you look at the photos below, you'll notice that I throw the cross while my blocking arm still has contact with his punching arm. As my upper body rotates with the cross, my blocking arm redirects his arm across his body, which in turn disrupts his balance and creates an opportunity for me to land my punch without obstruction. In the photos you'll also notice that as my opponent's jab comes at me, I move my lead arm to the outside of his jab. In order to pull this off, you must not only be able to spot the jab the instant your opponent throws it, but also react in the blink of an eye. If you hesitate with the block, your opponent will most likely punch you in the face. And if you hesitate to throw the cross once you've blocked the strike, your opponent will pull his arm back into his stance and you'll have lost a golden opportunity. Remember, you always want to make your opponent pay for attacking you.

Feijao and I are both in a standard stance, searching for an opening to attack.

Feijao throws a left jab toward my face. Having immediately spotted the punch, I move my left arm toward the outside of his left arm in preparation to block his strike.

I slide my left arm against the outside of Feijao's left arm. To redirect his punch, I move my left arm up and toward the outside of my body.

While my left arm still has contact with Feijao's left arm, I rotate my hips in a counterclockwise direction, come up onto the ball of my right foot, and throw a right cross toward his face. Notice how as I rotate, my left arm forces his left arm across his body, disrupting his balance and making it difficult for him to pull his arm back into his stance.

Having disrupted Feijao's balance, I continue with my counterclockwise rotation and land my right cross to the side of his face.

REAR ARM BLOCK TO LEAD HOOK

This technique is similar to the previous one, but instead of deflecting my opponent's jab using a lead arm block, I deflect his cross using a rear arm block. While my arm still has contact with his arm, I rotate my body and throw a lead hook. Once again, the rotating involved in my punch forces my opponent's arm across his body, disrupts his balance, and makes it very difficult for him to pull his arm back into his stance. This allows me to land a hook to his face without obstruction. If you look closely at the photos, you'll notice that as my opponent's cross comes at me, I move my head away from my centerline. Not only does this allow me to avoid taking a punch to the face, but it also makes it easier for me to move my rear arm to the outside of his punching arm. As with the previous technique, the only way to be successful with the initial block is to spot the punch coming. If you don't see it until it's halfway to your face, you won't have time to react with a block. To get better at reading your opponent's movements, spar as much as possible in the gym.

Feijao and I are both in a standard stance, searching for an opening to attack.

Feijao throws a right cross at my face. Having immediately spotted the punch, I shift my weight onto my left leg, rotate my hips and shoulders in a counterclockwise direction, and move my right arm to the outside of his right arm.

As Feijao's punch gets closer, I press my right arm against the outside of his right arm.

While my right arm still has contact with Feijao's right arm, I rotate my hips and shoulders in a clockwise direction and throw a left hook toward his face. Notice how my rotation forces his right arm across his body and disrupts his base.

Having disrupted Feijao's balance with my rotation, he is unable to quickly pull his right arm back into his stance and I land my hook to the side of his jaw.

BLOCK OVERHAND TO UPPERCUT COUNTER

This is the third technique in which I block a punch and then quickly rotate my hips to disrupt my opponent's balance, creating an opening for me to land a strike. In this particular scenario, my opponent throws an overhand right from close range. To block the punch, I utilize a lead outside block. While my arm still has contact with his arm, I rotate my hips and throw a rear uppercut. Due to my rotation, my opponent's punching arm gets forced to the outside of his body and I land a clean uppercut to his jaw. When studying the photos in the sequence below, it is important to notice how I flare the elbow of my blocking arm out to the side and drop my opposite shoulder. These movements not only allow me to effectively block the strike, but they also set my hips up to throw a more powerful right uppercut.

Feijao and I are in standard stances, searching for an opening to attack.

Feijao throws an overhand right toward my head, and immediately I elevate my left arm to block the punch.

Dropping my right shoulder and elevating my left elbow, Feijao's overhand slides up my forearm, drastically reducing its power. If you keep your arm vertical instead of angling your elbow out to the side, the impact of your opponent's punch is much greater.

While my left arm still has contact with Feijao's right arm, I rotate my body in a counterclockwise direction and drop my right hand in preparation for the uppercut. Notice how my rotation has forced his right arm toward the outside of his body, creating a clear path for the uppercut.

Having disrupted Feijao's balance with my rotation, I land an uppercut to his chin.

BLOCK OVERHAND TO KNEE

The scenario presented below is similar to the one in the previous sequence—my opponent and I are standing in close range, we have the same foot forward, and he throws an overhand right. However, instead of blocking his punch with my lead arm and throwing a rear uppercut, I block the overhand using both of my arms and throw a rear knee. To be successful with this technique, you must react to the punch as it's being thrown. The instant your opponent launches the overhand, elevate your arms and rotate your body to face the punch. The rotation is key because it spring-loads your hips and sets you up to throw a powerful knee. Although below I show the block and the knee strike as two separate steps for clarity purposes, both should be done almost simultaneously. The goal is to block the overhand and then use the rotation of your body to land the knee before your opponent can pull his arm back into his stance. In addition to developing the proper timing, you must also master this particular block. If you look at the third step below, you'll notice that my lead arm absorbs the majority of the impact while my rear arm catches my opponent's biceps for control.

Feijao and I are fighting in close range. Both of us are in standard stances, searching for an opening to attack.

Feijao throws a right overhand punch toward my head. Immediately I elevate my arms and begin turning into the punch by rotating in a counterclockwise direction.

I continue to rotate in a counterclockwise direction so that my shoulders are square with Feijao's approaching punch. This allows me to catch his punch using both of my arms. Notice how I absorb the majority of the impact with my left arm and catch his right biceps with my right arm.

I continue to rotate my hips in a counterclockwise direction.

Before Feijao can pull his arm back into his fighting stance, I use my counterclockwise rotation to drive a powerful straight knee into his abdomen.

BLOCK LEAD HOOK TO ELBOW

This is an excellent technique to utilize when you and your opponent are standing in close range with the same foot forward and he throws a lead hook. To block the strike, rotate your hips away from the punch and execute a rear outside block. Once the punch lands, your hips will be spring-loaded due to your rotation. While your blocking arm still has contact with your opponent's punching arm, rotate your body in the opposite direction. This not only lets you throw a powerful uppercut elbow, but it also forces your opponent's arm away from his body, separating his guard and allowing you to land your elbow strike without obstruction.

Feijao and I are in close range. We are both in a southpaw stance, searching for an opening to attack.

Feijao throws a lead right hook. Immediately I rotate my body in a clockwise direction, come up onto the ball of my left foot, and execute a rear outside block by reaching my left hand toward the back of my head.

Continuing to rotate my body in a clockwise direction, I block Feijao's lead hook using a rear outside block. Notice how I have angled my left elbow slightly out to the side. This causes his arm to slip up my arm instead of crash directly into it, reducing the damage caused by the blow.

The instant I block Feijao's lead hook, I rotate my hips and shoulders in a counterclockwise direction and throw a right uppercut elbow into his jaw. Notice how I threw the strike before he had a chance to pull his arm back into his stance and reestablish his guard.

COUNTER HOOK WITH CROSS TO KICK

One of the primary goals in fighting is to hit your opponent with a counterattack every time he throws a strike. Punishing him in this manner not only breaks his rhythm and prevents him from launching effective combinations, but it also keeps you on the offensive. In this particular scenario, my opponent and I are standing in punching range with the same foot forward. He throws a rear hook, and I counter with a right cross. Straight punches are quicker than looping punches because they have to travel less distance, but the only way to land your strike first is if you spot your opponent's punch early. Preferably, you want to throw the cross the instant you see your opponent begin to rotate his hips and shoulders for the punch. When first starting out, it can be difficult to discern what strike your opponent will throw based on his body mechanics alone, but you'll develop this naturally over time through sparring. Once you perfect this technique, or any other counterstrike for that matter, it is always good to follow up with a strike or combination of strikes. Having just disrupted your opponent's rhythm and possibly knocked him off balance, there is no better time to do damage. In this scenario, I opt to follow my counter cross with a kick to my opponent's head.

TECHNICAL NOTE

For safety measures, always keep your opposite arm up to protect your face when executing this technique. Beating your opponent to the punch will zap most of the power out of his strike, but if your timing is off or your opponent throws an extremely powerful punch, you don't want to take an unnecessary hit to the chin.

SAME STANCE

Feijao and I are in southpaw stances, searching for an opening to attack.

Feijao throws a rear hook toward my face. Immediately I elevate my right arm to protect the right side of my face, rotate my hips in a clockwise direction, come up onto the ball of my left foot, and throw a left cross toward his face.

Keeping my right arm up, I land a left cross to Feijao's face and zap the power from his punch.

Having landed a powerful cross, my goal is to immediately follow up with another strike. Deciding to throw a kick to Feijao's head, I have two options. I can immediately throw the kick after the cross or I can reestablish my fighting stance and then throw the kick. The former is quicker, but the latter possesses more power. In this case, I decide to reestablish my fighting stance. I accomplish this by pulling my left arm back and rotating my hips in a counterclockwise direction.

Once I reestablish my fighting stance, I immediately rotate my hips in a clockwise direction, shift my weight onto my right leg, and come up onto the ball of my left foot.

Continuing to rotate my hips in a clockwise direction, I pivot on the ball of my right foot, lean back to counterbalance my weight, throw my left arm behind me to generate power, and launch a left kick at Feijao's head.

LEAD STOP BLOCK TO STRAIGHT KNEE

In this sequence, I counter my opponent's overhand right with a lead stop block, push him off balance, and then follow up with a straight knee to his midsection. For this technique to work, you must read your opponent's movements and drive your palm into his shoulder before he generates power for the punch. The goal is to stop the rotation of his shoulders, thereby zapping the punch of any power and slowing the forward progression of his arm. Unless your opponent leans dramatically forward with his punch, the lead stop block will usually force him off balance, which allows you to land a clean counterstrike. In this particular case, I choose to follow up with a knee strike to his guts.

Feijao and I are in standard stances, searching for an opening to attack.

Feijao throws an overhand right toward my head. Immediately I throw my left hand toward his right shoulder.

Before Feijao can rotate his shoulders in a counter-clockwise direction and generate power for his overhand right, I drive my left palm into his right shoulder. Not only does this prevent him from generating power with the strike, but it also prevents him from fully extending his right arm.

Still driving my left palm into Feijao's right shoulder, I shift my weight onto my left leg and lean forward. Notice how this pushes him backward and disrupts his balance.

Still with my left palm pressing into Feijao's right shoulder, I drive my right knee into his midsection.

STOP BLOCK / OUTSIDE BLOCK / ELBOW

A lot of times countering an opponent's punch using a stop block isn't enough to prevent his fist from reaching your face. In some cases, the stop block may simply slow his punch down. If you find yourself in this situation, you need to take countermeasures to ensure you don't get hit. If you look at the photos in the sequence below, you'll notice that I execute a lead stop block to counter my opponent's overhand right. Although I stripped power and speed from his strike, it wasn't enough to halt the forward progression of his fist. To avoid getting hit, I transition from a stop block to an outside block, catching his fist on my arm. While my blocking arm still has contact with my opponent's punching arm, I rotate my hips and throw a rear side elbow. Notice in the photos below how my rotation forces his punching arm to the outside of his body and clears a path for the elbow strike.

Feijao and I are in standard stances, searching for an opening to attack.

Feijao throws an overhand right toward my head. Having spotted his punch early, I execute a stop block by driving my left palm into his right shoulder.

With Feijao leaning forward and putting all of his weight behind his punch, the stop block zaps power from his overhand but does not stop the forward progression of his arm.

As Feijao follows through with his punch, I pull my left palm off his right shoulder.

As Feijao's looping punch closes in, I pull my left arm straight back.

I perform an outside block with my left arm to block Feijao's right punch.

While my left arm still has contact with Feijao's right arm, I rotate my hips in a counterclockwise direction, come up onto the ball of my right foot, and throw a right side elbow toward Feijao's face. Notice how my rotation has forced his right arm toward the outside of his body, clearing a path for my elbow strike.

Continuing to rotate my body in a counterclockwise direction, I land a powerful right side elbow to Feijao's face.

BLOCK ELBOW TO UPPERCUT ELBOW

When you're in clinching range, you must always be on the lookout for elbow strikes. It is important to understand how to defend against all the various elbows attacks, but the side elbow is the most commonly thrown because it's fast, powerful, and easy to execute. On the upside, it's an easy strike to block. To defend against a rear side elbow when you and your opponent are in the same stance, all you have to do is elevate your lead arm so that your triceps is parallel with the ground. The goal is to extend your arm outward and catch your opponent's strike before it has reached the halfway point to your face. Accomplishing this prevents your opponent from generating a significant amount of power, which in turn reduces the damage you take to your arm. If you attempt to block a side elbow using an outside block, your opponent has the full range of motion in which to generate power. Even though you're technically blocking his strike, it can still rattle your focus or knock you off balance. Once you block the side elbow utilizing the method laid out below, it's in your best interest to immediately follow up with a counterattack. In this sequence, I choose to throw an uppercut elbow between my opponent's arms and into his chin.

Feijao and I are in standard stances, searching for an opening to attack.

Feijao elevates his right arm in preparation to throw a side elbow.

As Feijao drives his right side elbow forward, I elevate my left arm so that my triceps is parallel with the mat and extend my arm forward. This allows me to catch his elbow with my forearm before he can generate a significant amount of power with his hips.

While my left arm still has contact with Feijao's right arm, I rotate my hips in a counterclockwise direction, come up onto the ball of my right foot, and drive an uppercut elbow between his arms.

Still rotating my hips in a counterclockwise direction, I drive a right uppercut elbow into Feijao's chin.

BLOCK ELBOW TO SIDE ELBOW

This sequence begins the same as the previous one—my opponent and I are fighting in close range with the same foot forward, he throws a rear side elbow, and I block his strike as it reaches the halfway mark to my face using my lead forearm. However, in this scenario my opponent has dropped his lead arm, leaving his face vulnerable. Instead of countering with an uppercut elbow, I counter with a rear side elbow, which is the most powerful of all elbow strikes because it follows the same horizontal path of your hips and shoulders.

1

Feijao and I are in standard stances, searching for an opening to attack.

2

Feijao elevates his right arm in preparation to throw a side elbow.

As Feijao drives his right side elbow forward, I elevate my left arm so that my triceps is parallel with the mat and extend my arm forward. This allows me to catch his elbow with my forearm before he can generate a significant amount of power with his hips.

Seeing that Feijao has dropped his right arm, leaving his face vulnerable, I immediately rotate my hips in a counterclockwise direction, come up onto the ball of my right foot, and throw a rear side-elbow toward his jaw.

Continuing to rotate my hips in a counterclockwise direction, I land a rear side elbow to Feijao's jaw.

BLOCK ELBOW TO LEAD SIDE ELBOW

This is the third sequence in which I block a rear side elbow using my lead arm. The difference in this scenario is that my opponent has an extremely tight defense, making it difficult for me to counter with either a rear uppercut elbow or a rear side elbow. With the goal of making my opponent pay every time he throws a strike, I follow the block with a lead side elbow strike. To accomplish this, I immediately force my opponent's rear arm downward using my lead hand after executing the block. At the same time, I elevate my lead elbow. By executing the block and the counter in one fluid movement, I clear a path for the lead side elbow. Although the lead side-elbow doesn't pack as much power as the rear side elbow, when you time this technique correctly, your opponent's face will still be moving forward, doubling the impact of your strike.

Feijao and I are in standard stances, searching for an opening to attack.

Feijao elevates his right arm in preparation to throw a side elbow.

As Feijao drives his right side elbow forward, I elevate my left arm so that my triceps is parallel with the mat and extend my arm forward. This allows me to catch his elbow with my forearm before he can generate a significant amount of power with his hips.

Immediately after blocking Feijao's strike, I drop my left hand over his right hand and elevate my left elbow.

I continue to drive Feijao's right arm downward using my left hand, while at the same time elevating my left elbow.

Having forced Feijao's right arm downward, the right side of his face is vulnerable to attack. To capitalize on this opening I've created, I rotate my hips in a clockwise direction, shift my weight onto my left leg, and throw a lead side elbow into his jaw.

LEAN-BACK JAB COUNTER

When you and your opponent have the same foot forward, you have several options for countering his jab. You can use the lean-back counter, the inside slip, and the inside slip parry. However, if you and your opponent have opposite feet forward, your options for countering his jab with a jab become limited. If you attempt to avoid the punch with an inside slip, not only will you be unable to counter with a jab, but you also put your face in the direct line of fire for your opponent's cross. Remember, you never want to move toward your opponent's power. With the inside slip ruled out, your best option is to utilize the lean-back counter or an outside slip, which I will cover later. To utilize the lean-back counter, move your head backward just far enough to avoid the punch and catch your opponent's fist in your rear palm. If you have a longer reach than your opponent, you can counter with a jab at the same time and disrupt his rhythm. If he has a reach advantage on you, then your best option is to throw your counter jab as he pulls his jab arm back into his stance.

Feijao is in a standard stance, and I'm in a southpaw stance. Both of us are searching for an opening to attack.

Feijao throws a left jab toward my face. To counter his punch, I shift a larger portion of my weight onto my left leg, lean my head back, and throw a right jab.

As Feijao's left arm reaches the end of its extension, his fist stops several inches short of my face due to my evasive maneuver. However, due to my superior reach, my fist collides with the side of his jaw. It is important to note that by countering with a jab as I lean back, I prevent Feijao from adding extra length to his jab by leaning or taking a step forward.

Landing my jab clean, Feijao is thrown off balance, creating an opportunity for me to follow up with a number of different strikes.

HAND TRAP / JAB / SIDE KICK

The lead hand trap is another excellent way to counter your opponent's jab when you're in opposite fighting stances. As his fist comes at you, slap his arm downward and to the inside using your lead hand. The movement is similar to the parry in that you catch his fist as it crosses your guard, but instead of using your rear hand, you use your lead hand. When done correctly, your opponent's fist will get redirected away from your face and body, allowing you to immediately counter with a jab of your own. As with all the previous countering techniques, the goal is to strike your target before your opponent can pull his arm back into his stance. The trick to being successful with this technique is not exaggerating the hand-trapping movement. Only maneuver your lead hand far enough away from your body to slap his arm off course. If you reach, your opponent will be able to catch on to your plan and launch an attack based upon your countermovement. As long as you catch his punch halfway in its extension, and then only redirect his arm enough to prevent his fist from hitting your head or body, your lead arm will be left in the perfect position from which to counter with a jab. In this sequence, I opt to follow the jab with a side kick to my opponent's midsection.

Feijao is in a standard stance, and I'm in a southpaw stance. Both of us are searching for an opening to attack.

Feijao throws a left jab at my face. As his fist comes at me, I redirect his punch away from my face by slapping his arm downward and to my left side using my right hand. Notice how my movement is very subtle—If you exaggerate the hand trap, your guard will fall, giving your opponent an opportunity to follow up with another strike such as a cross. Dropping your hand too far downward also makes it difficult to immediately follow up with a jab.

Before Feijao can pull his left arm back into his stance, I throw a right jab at his chin. It is important to note that I didn't pull my right arm into my body after executing the hand trap, but rather shot my fist straight forward. As long as you remain relaxed, you can generate a substantial amount of power in your jab from a short distance.

Keeping my right arm extended to maintain distance, I lean back and shift my weight onto my left leg.

Balancing on my left leg, I rotate my hips in a counterclockwise direction and lift my right knee toward my chest in preparation for a side kick.

Leaning backward to maintain my balance, I throw a right side kick into Feijao's abdomen.

COUNTER JAB WITH HAND TRAP / ELBOW

The hand trap I use in this sequence is similar to the hand trap I used in the previous sequence, but instead of slapping my opponent's jab off course and then countering with a jab, I use the hand trap to pin his arm to his body. This allows me to step my lead foot to the outside of his lead foot, closing the distance and obtaining a dominant angle of attack at the same time. Still keeping my opponent's arm trapped to his body with my lead hand, I land a devastating rear side elbow strike from close range. Due to the limited reach of the elbow strike, this technique is best utilized when your opponent throws his jab from punching range. It is also important that you execute the countermovement and attack in one fluid motion.

Feijao and I are standing within punching distance. He is in a standard stance, and I'm in a southpaw stance.

Feijao throws a left jab at my face. To counter his punch, I step my right foot to the outside of his left foot and sweep my right arm toward the left side of my body, catching his arm and redirecting it.

Continuing to sweep my right arm toward my left side, I redirect Feijao's punch and force his hips to turn in a clockwise direction. At the same time, I rotate my hips in a clockwise direction and elevate my left elbow.

Keeping Feijao's guard broken with my right hand, I rotate my hips in a clockwise direction and deliver a powerful left side elbow to his head.

OPPOSITE STANCE

COUNTER JAB WITH CROSS

While countering a jab using an inside slip works wonderfully when you and your opponent have the same foot forward, it's not your best option when you have opposite feet forward. In addition to moving directly into your opponent's power, it becomes impossible to fire back with a jab of your own. However, it's quite possible to evade his jab using an outside slip. Although the positioning of your body makes it difficult to counter with a jab, it becomes easy to counter with a cross. It's one of the most popular counterattacks in the book, and for good reason. The movements involved in executing the outside slip are almost identical to the movements involved in throwing a cross. Mechanically, they work flawlessly when combined. As when you counter the jab with a jab, the goal is to land the cross while your opponent's arm is just completing its extension. This is a very important counterattack to have in your arsenal, and I strongly suggest drilling it until it becomes second nature.

> **TECHNICAL NOTE**
>
> This same combination can also be employed when you and your opponent are in the same fighting stance, but instead of using it to counter his jab, you would use it to counter his cross.

Feijao is in a standard stance, and I'm in a southpaw stance. Both of us are looking for an opening to attack.

Feijao throws a left jab at my face. To counter, I take a small outward step with my right foot, dip my head toward my right side, and throw a left cross toward his face.

Due to my head movement, Feijao's jab slips by the left side of my face.

As Feijao fully extends his arm, I bend at the waist and deliver a powerful left cross to his chin.

OUTSIDE SLIP / REVERSE ELBOW

Earlier in the book I demonstrated how to throw the reverse back elbow, as well as how to use it in combination with other strikes. In this sequence, I show how it can be used to counter your opponent's jab when the two of you are in opposite fighting stances. To execute this technique, employ an outside slip as your opponent throws a jab at your face. This allows you to step your rear foot forward and throw a reverse back elbow up between his arms and strike his chin. For the best results, you want to land the elbow before your opponent can pull his arm back into his stance, which means becoming very familiar with the movements involved.

Feijao is in a standard stance, and I'm in a southpaw stance. Both of us are looking for an opening to attack.

Feijao throws a left jab at my face. To counter, I dip my head toward my right side.

Continuing to slip my head toward my right side, I drop my level by bending at the knees.

As Feijao's jab slips by my head, I increase my elevation by straightening my legs, rotate my hips in a clockwise direction, and move my left arm toward my right side in preparation for the elbow strike.

Before Feijao can pull his jab arm back into his stance, I step my left foot forward and drive my left elbow upward toward his chin. Notice how my left elbow is underneath his left arm. In order for this technique to work, you must launch your elbow strike before your opponent can bring his arm back into his body and reestablish his guard.

Dipping my head toward my right side, I slide my entire left shoulder underneath Feijao's left arm and drive the tip of my elbow upward into his chin. Notice how I have raised my right arm to protect my head.

COUNTER CROSS WITH SPINNING BACK FIST

In this sequence I demonstrate how to counter a cross with a spinning back fist when you and your opponent are in opposite fighting stances. If you look at the photos below, you'll notice that I not only step back to avoid my opponent's punch, but I also use my rear arm to redirect his punch to the inside of his body, which disrupts his balance. With my opponent having to reestablish his base before he can shoot in for a takedown or wrap me up in a body lock, I step back into him and safely execute the spinning back fist. However, this technique becomes a lot riskier when you hesitate between steps. For the best results, you want to complete your rotation and execute the spinning back fist in one fluid motion. As I mentioned before, you don't have to be as accurate with the spinning back fist as you do with other strikes. Hitting your opponent with either your fist or forearm will cause significant damage.

Feijao is in a standard stance, and I'm in a southpaw stance. Both of us are searching for an opening to attack.

Feijao rotates his hips in a counterclockwise direction and throws a right cross toward my face.

3

To avoid Feijao's cross, I step my right foot back. Next, I rotate my hips in a clockwise direction, come up onto the ball of my left foot, and use my left hand to redirect his right arm toward the inside of his body.

4

Having disrupted Feijao's balance by redirecting his right arm toward the inside of his body, I step my left foot to the outside of his left foot and rotate my body in a clockwise direction.

5

Pivoting on my left foot, I slide my right foot along a circular path toward Feijao's left foot. At the same time, I elevate my right elbow in preparation for the spinning back fist.

6

Rotating my hips and shoulders in a clockwise direction, I whip my right arm along a circular path and strike the side of Feijao's face.

LEAD ARM BLOCK TO CROSS COUNTER

In this sequence, I deflect my opponent's right cross with a lead arm block and then redirect his arm to the inside of his body by throwing a left cross. Reading your opponent's movements and then reacting before he extends his arm is key with this technique. If you look at the photos below, you'll notice that as my opponent begins to throw his punch I rotate my body away from his strike and move my lead arm to the outside of his arm. This allows me to deflect his strike away from my face. However, my goal is to make my opponent pay for trying to punch me, so while my arm still has contact with his arm, I rotate my body into his punch and throw a cross. Notice how my rotation forces his arm toward the inside of his body, which disrupts his balance and clears a pathway for the cross.

Feijao is in a standard stance, and I'm in a southpaw stance. Both of us are searching for an opening to attack.

Feijao throws a right cross toward my face. Immediately I rotate my hips in a counter-clockwise direction and move my right arm to the outside of his right arm.

By slightly rotating my hips in a clockwise direction, my right arm slides against Feijao's arm and deflects his fist away from my face.

While my right arm still has contact with Feijao's right arm, I rotate my hips in a clockwise direction, come up onto the ball of my left foot, and throw a left cross toward his face. Notice how my rotation forces his right arm toward the inside of his body. This disrupts his balance, makes it difficult for him to pull his arm back into his stance, and clears a path for my left cross.

Continuing to rotate my hips in a clockwise direction, I land a left cross to Feijao's jaw.

ARM BLOCK / SIDE STEP / UPPERCUT

This is another effective way to block and counter the cross when you and your opponent are in opposite fighting stances. Just as I did in the previous sequence, I rotate my body away from the strike and move my lead arm to the outside of my opponent's punch the instant I see him gearing up to attack with a cross. However, in this scenario I position my lead arm at a forty-five-degree angle in relation to the ground and drop my elevation by bending at the knees. My goal is still to block my opponent's punch, but instead of deflecting his arm toward the side, I deflect it upward. Keeping my opponent's rear arm elevated with my lead arm, I step my rear foot diagonally forward, rotate my hips and shoulders, and drive a rear uppercut underneath his extended arm and into his chin. As with all counters, quick reactions and fluid movements are the keys to success. If you fail to land the uppercut before your opponent pulls his arm back into his stance, you'll likely punch his elbow instead of his chin.

Feijao is in a standard stance, and I'm in a southpaw stance. Both of us are searching for an opening to attack.

Feijao throws a right cross at my face. Immediately I rotate my body in a counterclockwise direction, move my right arm to the outside of his right arm, and drop my elevation by bending slightly at the knees. Notice how instead of keeping my blocking arm vertical, I have positioned it at a forty-five-degree angle in relation to the ground.

As Feijao's right fist nears my face, I slide my right arm against his right arm and deflect it upward.

Pushing Feijao's right arm upward using my right arm, I take a diagonal step forward with my left foot.

Still keeping Feijao's right arm elevated using my right arm, I rotate my body in a clockwise direction, pivot on my left foot, and throw a left uppercut toward his chin.

Continuing to rotate in a clockwise direction, I throw a left uppercut underneath Feijao's right arm and strike his chin.

LEVEL CHANGE / UPPERCUT ELBOW

There are several ways to evade the cross when you and your opponent are squared off in opposite fighting stances. Earlier in the book I demonstrated how to accomplish this using an inside slip, an outside slip, and leaning your head back. In this sequence, I demonstrate how to avoid your opponent's cross by dropping your level and moving your head to the outside of the punch. It's not as fluid as the options already covered, but it sets you up perfectly to land an uppercut elbow to your opponent's jaw. The goal is to execute the countermovements and come upward with the elbow before your opponent can pull his arm back into his stance. The upward elbow by itself isn't that powerful of a technique, but when combined with the upward momentum of your body, it has knockout potential.

Feijao and I are standing within punching range. He is in a standard stance, and I'm in a southpaw stance. Both of us are looking for an opening to attack.

Feijao throws a right cross at my face. To evade his strike, I take a small outward step with my left foot, shift a larger portion of my weight onto my left leg, move my body toward my left side, and drop my elevation by bending my knees and sinking my hips. Notice how even though I have moved my body toward my left, my upper body is still erect. If you lean, you compromise your base and balance.

3

Continuing to drop my level and shift my body toward my left side, Feijao's cross glides past my head.

4

Before Feijao can pull his right arm back into his stance, I explode upward off my legs, driving my right shoulder toward his right arm.

5

Coming all the way back up into my fighting stance, I catch Feijao's right arm on my right shoulder, further breaking down his guard. At the same time, I throw my right elbow upward toward his chin.

6

Shifting my weight onto my right leg, I slightly rotate my hips in a counterclockwise direction, lean forward, and drive my right elbow upward into Feijao's jaw. Notice how although I'm leaning forward, my upper body is still centered over my right leg, allowing me to maintain balance should I miss my strike.

OPPOSITE STANCE

LEVEL CHANGE / OVER-THE-TOP ELBOW

In this sequence, I demonstrate how to counter an overhand punch with an over-the-top elbow when you and your opponent are in opposite fighting stances. If you look at the photos below, you'll notice that the instant my opponent begins to throw the overhand, I drop my level, which takes my head off line from his punch. Without hesitating, I drive forward and throw an over-the-top elbow into the gap created by my opponent's wide punch. The over-the-top elbow is a powerful strike when thrown by itself, but when combined with your forward momentum, it can have devastating results. As with all countering techniques, timing and a keen sense of distance is mandatory.

Feijao and I are in close range. He is in a standard stance, and I'm in a southpaw stance. Both of us are looking for an opening to attack.

Feijao throws an overhand right toward my head. Immediately I drop my elevation by bending at the knees.

Continuing to drop my level, I rotate my hips in a clockwise direction, come up onto the ball of my left foot, and throw a left over-the-top elbow into the open space created by Feijao's wide punch.

As Feijao's overhand follows a circular path toward my face, I continue to rotate my hips in a clockwise direction and throw my linear over-the-top elbow toward his face.

Bending at the hips, I strike Feijao in the side of the jaw with my over-the-top elbow. By landing the powerful strike, I have greatly reduced the power behind his strike. However, if he had managed to continue with his punch, it would have glided over the top of my head due to my level change.

COUNTER CROSS WITH REAR SIDE ELBOW

In this sequence, I demonstrate how to counter a cross with a rear side elbow when you and your opponent are in opposite fighting stances. If you look at the photos below, you'll see that as my opponent extends his right arm to deliver the cross, I step my lead foot to the outside of his lead foot. This serves two purposes. Most importantly, it moves my head away from the path of the punch, eliminating any chance of getting hit. Secondly, it creates enough space to counter with a powerful rear side-elbow. To deliver a knockout blow, use the momentum of the side step to add power to the side-elbow. Like the other counters, the goal is to land the counterstrike as your opponent's arm reaches the end of its extension.

Feijao and I are in close range. He's in a standard stance, and I'm in a southpaw stance. We're both looking for an opening to attack.

Feijao throws a right cross at my face. To evade his strike, I take a small outward step with my right foot, rotate my hips in a clockwise direction, come up onto the ball of my left foot, and shift my body toward my right side.

As Feijao's cross slips past my head, I rotate my body in a clockwise direction, shift my weight onto my right leg, and throw a left side elbow toward his face.

Continuing to rotate in a clockwise direction, I connect with a left side elbow just as Feijao's right arm becomes fully extended. If you hesitate between slipping the punch and throwing the elbow, your opponent will be able to pull his cross arm back into his stance and reestablish his guard.

OPPOSITE STANCE

OUTSIDE SLIP / INSIDE SLIP / UPPERCUT

When your opponent throws a strike, the goal is to counter with a strike of your own to shatter his rhythm and create an opening to launch a devastating combination. I've offered numerous counterattacks to achieve this goal, but sometimes beating your opponent to the punch on his first strike isn't an option. If you can't get off a counterstrike before he throws his secondary attack, evading both strikes and then countering is your next best option. In the sequence below, my opponent throws a jab/cross combination, often referred to as the traditional one-two. To evade the jab, I execute an outside slip, and to evade the cross, I utilize an inside slip. As my opponent's cross sails past my head, I switch to offense by throwing a rear uppercut to his ribs. It is important to mention that going to the body is not your only option in this situation—you could just as well throw a rear uppercut to his face. The strike you choose should be based on personal preference, the body positioning of you and your opponent, and the available openings.

Feijao and I are in close range. He is in a standard stance, and I'm in a southpaw stance. Both of us are looking for an opening to attack.

Feijao throws a left jab toward my face. Immediately I begin rotating my hips in a clockwise direction.

Continuing to rotate my hips and shoulders in a clockwise direction, I come up onto the ball of my left foot and dip my head toward my right side. Notice how Feijao's entire left side is vulnerable.

Before I can launch an attack, Feijao begins to throw a right cross.

I rotate my hips in a counterclockwise direction.

Continuing to rotate my hips in a counterclockwise direction, I shift a larger portion of my weight onto my left leg and dip my head toward my left side.

Still rotating my hips in a counterclockwise direction and dipping my head toward my left side, Feijao's cross misses its target.

Rotating my hips in a clockwise direction, I catch Feijao's right arm with my right forearm and force it toward my right side. My goal behind this action is to throw off his balance and base, making it difficult for him to follow up with another strike.

Continuing to rotate my hips in a clockwise direction, I force Feijao's right arm farther toward my right side. At the same time, I come up onto the ball of my left foot and drop my left arm in preparation to throw an uppercut to his ribs.

Generating power with the rotation of my hips, I drive a left uppercut into Feijao's midsection.

INSIDE SLIP / OUTSIDE SLIP / HOOK

When you fight a worthy opponent, the chances are the majority of his attacks will be combinations rather than single strikes. Again, it's best to evade his first strike and counter at the same time, stopping him dead in his tracks before he can even get started, but as I have already mentioned, this isn't always possible. In this sequence, my opponent begins his combination with a cross, which I evade using an inside slip. Before I have a chance to counter, he throws a jab, which I evade using an outside slip. Since I still haven't been able to counter, he throws a rear hook. Now three punches deep into my opponent's combination, I see my chance. As I slip underneath his rear hook, I throw a lead hook to his jaw, shattering his rhythm. Immediately I switch from defense to offense. Drilling to counter a combination of strikes such as this one is key because it mimics a real fight and allows you to flow from one evasive tactic to the next until you spot an opening to attack.

Feijao and I are in close range. He is in a standard stance, and I'm in a southpaw stance. Both of us are looking for an opening to attack.

Feijao throws a right cross toward my face. To evade his punch, I immediately begin to lower my elevation by bending at the knees.

Continuing to lower my elevation by bending at the knees, I dip my head toward my left side. Due to my evasive maneuvers, Feijao's cross sails past my head.

4

As Feijao pulls his right arm back into his stance, I increase my elevation by straightening my legs and torso.

5

I return to my original fighting stance.

6

Before I can launch an attack, Feijao throws a left jab at my face. To evade his punch, I again drop my elevation by bending at the knees. However, this time I shift my upper body toward my right side.

As Feijao pulls his left arm back into his stance, he begins to throw a right hook. To evade and counter his punch, I begin rotating my hips in a counterclockwise direction and throw a right hook toward his face.

Continuing to rotate my hips in a counterclockwise direction, I drop my elevation by bending at the knees and extend my right hook toward Feijao's face.

Due to my evasive maneuvers, Feijao's right hook sails over the top of my head. At the same moment, I land my right hook to the side of his jaw.

LEAD CHECK / KICK / KNEE

As I mentioned in the introduction to this section, you want to answer every one of your opponent's strikes with a counter-attack. This is especially true with kicks. When you check a kick, it takes longer for your opponent to pull his leg back into his stance than it does for you to drop your foot back to the mat. If you get into the habit of aggressively moving forward after each kick you check, you'll land clean strikes a large portion of the time and frequently knock your opponent off balance, which creates an opportunity to follow up with yet more strikes. In order to become a master in this arena of combat, it is important that you practice countering after checking both mid and high kicks, but in the beginning you'll want to focus on the rear outside low kick because it is the most common kick thrown in MMA. If you look at the photos in the sequence below, you'll notice that I counter my opponent's rear outside low kick with a left lead check. Immediately after, I drop my foot to the mat and return fire with a right low kick of my own. The reason I choose the exact same kick that my opponent threw is because the majority of his weight is still resting on his lead leg. It's also important to notice how I place my right hand on his shoulder as I counter. This allows me to gauge distance and keeps my opponent off balance as I move forward with the kick. In this particular sequence, I do not pull my leg back into my original fighting stance after crashing my shin into my opponent's thigh. Instead, I keep my leg forward and plant my foot to the outside of my opponent's lead leg. This puts me into a perfect position to assume the Muay Thai clinch and drive a powerful knee into his midsection.

1

Feijao and I are in standard stances, searching for an opening to attack.

2

Feijao shifts his weight onto his lead leg and begins rotating his hips, alerting me to the fact that he's about to throw a rear low kick to the outside of my lead leg. Immediately I shift my weight onto my right leg and begin elevating my left leg.

Elevating my left knee to waist level, Feijao's leg crashes into my shin.

I drop my left foot straight to the mat, shift my weight onto my left leg, rotate my hips in a counterclockwise direction, come up onto the ball of my right foot, and shoot my right hand toward Feijao's left shoulder.

Driving my right palm into Feijao's left shoulder to prevent him from recovering his balance after the kick, I rotate my hips in a counterclockwise direction and pivot on my left foot.

6

Continuing to rotate my hips in a counterclockwise direction, I throw rear low round kick into the outside of Feijao's left thigh.

7

Instead of pulling my right leg back and reestablishing my original fighting stance, I drop my right foot toward the outside of Feijao's left foot.

8

Planting my right foot to the outside of Feijao's left foot, I cup my right hand around the back of his neck and slide my right elbow toward the center of his chest.

Rotating my body in a clockwise direction, I come up onto the ball of my left foot and establish the Muay Thai clinch by cupping my left hand around the back of Feijao's head. Notice how I'm pinching his head between my elbows to prevent him from escaping.

Pulling Feijao's head down using my arms, I drive a left straight knee toward his midsection.

Still pulling Feijao's head down using my arms, I arc back and drive a left straight knee into his midsection.

CROSS CHECK / ELBOW / UPPERCUT-HOOK

In this sequence my opponent and I are in opposite fighting stances, and he throws a rear round kick to the inside of my lead leg. Due to our positioning, I block his kick using a lead cross check. As always, my goal is to make my opponent pay for attacking me, so instead of dropping my foot straight down to the mat, I step my lead foot forward, putting me into close range. While my opponent is still trying to reestablish his stance, I rotate my body and throw a rear side elbow to his face. It is important to note that the only way to land the side elbow clean is if your opponent drops his hands, but this is quite common, even among elite strikers. Once I've rattled my opponent with the elbow, I pull my rear arm back into my stance, rotate my hips in the opposite direction, and throw a punch with my lead hand. With my opponent's guard still low, I could have chosen an uppercut or a hook, but in this situation I chose to blend the two punches together. I throw my lead fist at an upward angle just as I would when throwing an uppercut, but I rotate my hips and shoulder just as I would when throwing a hook. A dangerous fighter is one who can attack from any angle. In order to accomplish that goal, sometimes you need to combine two strikes into one.

Feijao is in a standard stance, and I'm in a southpaw stance. Both of us are searching for an opening to attack.

Feijao throws a rear round kick toward the inside of my lead leg.

I block Feijao's rear low round kick using a lead cross check.

Instead of dropping my right foot straight down to the mat, I move into close range by stepping my right foot forward.

While Feijao is still trying to reestablish his fighting stance, I rotate my hips in a clockwise direction and throw a rear side elbow toward the side of his face. Notice how I have kept my right arm up to protect myself from strikes.

Still rotating my hips in a clockwise direction, I strike Feijao in the jaw with a rear side elbow.

Having stunned Feijao with the rear side elbow, I pull my left arm back into my stance, rotate my hips in a counterclockwise direction, and drop my right arm in preparation for the punch.

Still rotating my hips in a counterclockwise direction, I throw a punch that is a combination of an uppercut and a hook. It's like an uppercut in that it follows an upward trajectory, and it's like a hook in that I turn my hand over so it faces the mat.

CATCHING A MID-RANGE ROUND KICK

Checking your opponent's mid kicks is usually the best way to ensure minimal damage, but catching a mid kick opens up a lot more counterstriking opportunities. It allows you to keep your opponent's leg trapped tightly to your side and attack with a number of different strikes. It allows you to toss his leg to the side and disrupt his balance, making him an easy target. It also allows you to kick out the one leg he's balancing on and take him to the ground. However, to effectively catch a mid kick there are a few rules you must follow. The first is to never reach. If you reach for your opponent's leg every time he throws a mid kick, he'll catch on to the pattern. He might fake a mid kick and instead throw a superman punch. He might also switch things up by throwing a kick to your head. The second rule is to keep your opposite hand up to protect your face. The instant you catch your opponent's leg, he's going to do everything in his power to escape, and often this includes bouncing on one leg and firing jabs into your face. The third rule is to counter as quickly as possible. As I just mentioned, your opponent won't hang out in this position forever, so you want to quickly use your control to off-balance him and follow up with a counterattack. There are a huge number of attacking options at your disposal, but in this section I include the ones that have worked best for me. Personally, I catch kicks quite frequently, but it is important to remember that it's somewhat of a dangerous technique. There are, however, things you can do to minimize the danger, such as side-stepping in the same direction the kick is heading just prior to impact and partially blocking the kick with your far hand. When you manage to do both, the chances of your opponent's mid kick causing you damage drop significantly.

Feijao and I are in southpaw stances, searching for an opening to attack.

Feijao rotates his hips in a clockwise direction and throws a rear round kick toward my midsection. Immediately I begin moving my left palm toward the right side of my body to help absorb the impact of the blow.

Just prior to Feijao's kick landing, I drive my left palm into his leg to minimize the impact. Next, I immediately wrap my right arm tightly around his leg to secure it to my side. From here, I will immediately launch a counterattack.

CATCHING A LOW OUTSIDE ROUND KICK

To catch a kick aimed at the outside of your lead leg, you want to drop your level by bending at the knees just prior to the kick landing. With your legs angled outward, your opponent's kick will slide up your thigh, making his leg easier to trap. If your opponent's kick doesn't slide up to your waist, hook your hand around his ankle and pull his leg up to your side. Once accomplished, immediately follow up with a counterattack. The most important aspect about this technique is not dropping your level too early. If you drop your level just as your opponent's foot leaves the canvas, he might pick up on your intentions and redirect his kick to your head or midsection. He might even pull his kick back and throw a punch instead.

Feijao and I are in southpaw stances, searching for an opening to attack.

Feijao shifts his weight onto his lead leg and begins rotating in a clockwise direction, alerting me to the fact that he is about to throw a rear round kick.

3

Realizing Feijao is throwing a round kick to my lead leg, I decide to catch his kick. To accomplish this, I drop my level by bending at the knees and hook my right arm over his right leg the instant it lands. Notice how I have kept my left hand up to protect myself from strikes.

4

Due to how I angled my legs outward, Feijao's left leg slides up my right thigh, allowing me to hook my right hand around his ankle.

5

Using my hook on Feijao's left ankle, I pull his leg upward and secure it tightly to my side.

CATCH KICK TO LEG DESTRUCTION

When you catch the kick of a taller opponent, it can be difficult to throw a counterstrike to his body or head due to the distance between you. When faced with such a situation, targeting his trapped leg with a knee strike is a good option. In this sequence, I elevate my rear knee to the inside of my opponent's leg, just as I would when throwing a side knee. However, instead of sweeping my knee horizontally into my opponent's trapped leg, I sweep it horizontally and downward. This allows me to put my weight into the strike and drive my shin down into my opponent's thigh. To maintain distance while executing this technique, I reach my rear arm forward and place my hand on my opponent's lead shoulder.

I've caught Feijao's right round kick. To maintain distance between us and keep him off balance, I place my right hand on his right shoulder.

I elevate my right knee to the inside of Feijao's right leg.

I sweep my right knee downward and to my left, striking Feijao's thigh just above his kneecap with my shin.

CATCH KICK TO STRAIGHT KNEE

Sometimes when you catch your opponent's kick, he'll lean forward to maintain his balance. This is especially true with fighters who have poor flexibility in their hamstrings and groin. When faced with this scenario, a good option is to wrap your free hand around the back of your opponent's neck, pull his head toward the mat, and drive a powerful knee upward into either his midsection or head. The most important aspect with this technique is maintaining your grip on your opponent's leg as you throw your knee strike.

I've caught Feijao's left round kick. Notice how I've kept my left arm up to protect my face.

Maintaining my grip on Feijao's leg with my right hand, I rotate my body in a clockwise direction.

Continuing to rotate in a clockwise direction, I come up onto the ball of my left foot, reach my left hand around the left side of Feijao's head, and cup my palm on the back of his neck.

Using my left hand, I drive Feijao's head toward the mat.

Still driving Feijao's head toward the mat, I throw a rear straight knee into his midsection.

CATCH KICK TO DOWNWARD ELBOW

This is another technique that you can utilize when you catch the kick of a taller opponent. Instead of sweeping a side knee into his captured leg, drop a rear downward elbow into the soft flesh just above his kneecap. When you land the strike hard enough, you can render your opponent's leg useless for the remainder of the fight.

1

Having caught Feijao's right round kick, I place my right hand on his right shoulder to maintain distance.

2

I elevate my right hand above my head.

3

Bending forward at the waist, I drive the tip of my right elbow downward into the soft flesh just above Feijao's right kneecap.

CATCH KICK TO UPPERCUT ELBOW

The uppercut elbow is another excellent technique to employ when you catch your opponent's kick. To use this technique effectively, you want to pull your opponent's trapped leg backward to throw him off balance and get his body moving toward you. At the same time, step your rear foot forward and throw an uppercut elbow. The goal is to land the elbow while his momentum is still moving into you, increasing the impact of the strike. What makes this technique so effective is that it's a short movement, making it extremely quick to execute. It's also a difficult strike for your opponent to block because your elbow travels at an upward angle between his arms.

Having caught Feijao's round kick, I place my right hand on his right shoulder to maintain distance.

I pull Feijao's right leg backward using my left hand. At the same time, I step my right foot forward to close the distance between us.

Reaching my right hand behind my head, I drive an uppercut elbow into Feijao's jaw.

CATCH KICK TO REAR ELBOW

When you catch an opponent's kick and push him backward, the chances are he will press back into you to counterbalance his weight. In this sequence, I use this reaction to my advantage. Having caught my opponent's kick, I place my free hand on his shoulder and step my rear leg forward to close the distance between us. Once in close range, I extend my free arm into his shoulder and drive him backward. While there is distance between us, I retract my free hand and use it to latch on to my opponent's trapped leg, freeing my rear arm. As my opponent drives back into me to maintain his balance, I rotate my hips and shoulders and throw a rear side elbow into his face.

Having caught Feijao's round kick, I place my right hand on his right shoulder to maintain distance and keep him off balance.

Maintaining my grip on Feijao's right leg, I step my right foot forward.

I drive my right hand into Feijao's right shoulder, forcing him backward.

Having created distance with my shove, I retract my right arm, grab Feijao's trapped leg using my right hand, and release my left grip.

As Feijao drives back into me to maintain his balance, I rotate my hips and shoulders in a clockwise direction, come up onto the ball of my left foot, lean forward, and drive a powerful rear side elbow into his jaw.

CATCH KICK TO SPINNING BACK ELBOW

When you catch your opponent's kick, most of the time he'll expect you to throw linear attacks such as a cross or a knee to the midsection. Employing a spinning back elbow is an excellent way to catch him off guard. However, in order for this technique to work, you must be fast and aggressive with your movements. The more you hesitate between the steps, the more you expose yourself to possible counterattacks. It is also very important that you maintain control of your opponent's leg as you execute your turn. Switching your grips can be a difficult to get the hang of, so I recommend practicing this technique thoroughly in the gym before attempting to use it in competition.

1

I've caught Feijao's left round kick.

2

Elevating my left arm to protect my head, I rotate my hips and shoulders in a clockwise direction and come up onto the ball of my left foot.

Continuing to rotate in a clockwise direction, I step my left foot forward toward Feijao's trapped leg. As my foot touches down, I hook my left arm underneath his captured leg.

Maintaining my left hook on Feijao's captured leg, I continue to rotate my body in a clockwise direction, slide my right foot along a circular path toward Feijao's planted leg, and elevate my right elbow.

Still rotating in a clockwise direction, I throw a spinning back elbow into Feijao's face.

REDIRECT KICK TO REAR ELBOW

In this sequence I catch my opponent's kick just as I did in the previous ones, but instead of immediately launching a counterattack, I sink my hips back, move his leg to the opposite side of my body, and then throw his leg forcibly to the side to disrupt his balance. If you look at the photos below, you'll notice that this crosses my opponent's legs and destroy his defenses. Before he can reestablish his fighting stance, I capitalize on my dominant angle by throwing a rear side elbow to his face.

Having caught Feijao's round kick, I place my right hand on his right shoulder to maintain distance and keep him off balance.

I retract my right arm and grab Feijao's right leg using my right hand.

Sinking my hips backs, I use both of my grips on Feijao's ankle to move his leg toward my right side.

Releasing my left grip, I force Feijao's right leg toward my right side using my right hand.

I toss Feijao's leg toward my right side.

Having disrupted Feijao's balance, I rotate my hips and shoulders in a clockwise direction, come up onto the ball of my left foot, and throw a rear side elbow into his jaw.

VICTORY BELT

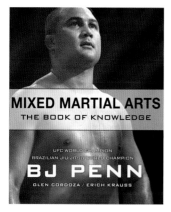

MIXED MARTIAL ARTS

BJ PENN

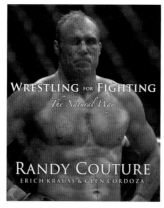

WRESTLING FOR FIGHTING

RANDY COUTURE

FEDOR

FEDOR
EMELIANENKO

MASTERING THE RUBBER GUARD

EDDIE BRAVO

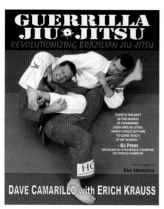

GUERRILLA JIU-JITSU

DAVE CAMARILLO

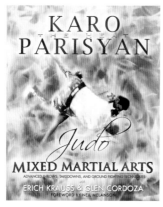

JUDO FOR MIXED MARTIAL ARTS

KARO PARISYAN

THE X-GUARD

MARCELO GARCIA

MASTERING THE TWISTER

EDDIE BRAVO

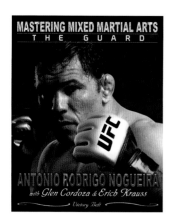

MASTERING MIXED MARTIAL ARTS

ANTONIO RODRIGO
NOGUEIRA

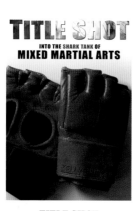

TITLE SHOT

KELLY CRIGGER

**MASTERING THE
RUBBER GUARD (DVD)**

EDDIE BRAVO

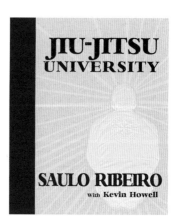

JIU-JITSU UNIVERSITY

SAULO RIBEIRO

MIXED MARTIAL ARTS INSTRUCTION MANUAL

RELATED PROJECTS BY ANDERSON SILVA

Mixed Martial Arts Instruction Manual: THE CLINCH
by Anderson Silva with Erich Krauss & Glen Cordoza

Boxing for Mixed Martial Arts (DVD)
by Anderson Silva with Brian Rule, Erich Krauss & Glen Cordoza

Muay Thai for Mixed Martial Arts (DVD)
by Anderson Silva with Brian Rule, Erich Krauss & Glen Cordoza

The Clinch for Mixed Martial Arts (DVD)
by Anderson Silva with Brian Rule, Erich Krauss & Glen Cordoza

Takedowns & Takedown Defense (DVD)
by Anderson Silva with Brian Rule, Erich Krauss & Glen Cordoza

RELATED BOOKS FROM VICTORY BELT

Fedor: The Fighting System of the World's Undisputed King of MMA
    by Fedor Emelianenko with Glen Cordoza & Erich Krauss

Mastering the Rubber Guard by Eddie Bravo with Erich Krauss & Glen Cordoza

Mastering the Rubber Guard DVD by Eddie Bravo with the Victory Belt Staff

Guerrilla Jiu-Jitsu: Revolutionizing Brazilian Jiu-Jitsu by Dave Camarillo with Erich Krauss

Mixed Martial Arts: The Book of Knowledge by BJ Penn with Glen Cordoza & Erich Krauss

Wrestling for Fighting: The Natural Way by Randy Couture with Erich Krauss & Glen Cordoza

Mastering the Twister by Eddie Bravo with Erich Krauss & Glen Cordoza

Judo for Mixed Martial Arts by Karo Parisyan with Erich Krauss & Glen Cordoza

Title Shot: In the Shark Tank of Mixed Martial Arts by Kelly Crigger

COMING SOON FROM VICTORY BELT

Brazilian Jiu-Jitsu Book of Knowledge: THE GUARD
    by BJ Penn with Glen Cordoza, Erich Krauss & Dave Camarillo

Brazilian Jiu-Jitsu Book of Knowledge: PASSING THE GUARD
    by BJ Penn with Glen Cordoza, Erich Krauss & Dave Camarillo

Brazilian Jiu-Jitsu Book of Knowledge: MOUNT, SIDE CONTROL, AND BACK
    by BJ Penn with Glen Cordoza, Erich Krauss & Dave Camarillo

Mastering Mixed Martial Arts by Antonio Rodrigo Nogueira with Erich Krauss & Glen Cordoza

From Wrestling to MMA by Matt Lindland with Glen Cordoza & Erich Krauss

Arm Drags and Back Attacks by Marcelo Garcia with Erich Krauss & Glen Cordoza

Ultimate Competition Jiu-Jitsu by Andre Galvao with Kevin Howell

Karate for Mixed Martial Arts by Lyoto Machida with Erich Krauss & Glen Cordoza

Jiu-Jitsu University by Saulo Ribeiro with Kevin Howell

The Natural Workout by Randy Couture with James Smith, Erich Krauss, & Neil Melanson

Guerrilla Knifefighting by Jered Feierabend & Dave Camarillo with Erich Krauss

Triangles from the Guard by Neil Melanson with Erich Krauss

ABOUT THE AUTHORS

ANDERSON SILVA IS THE UFC MIDDLE-WEIGHT CHAMPION OF THE WORLD. HE IS CONSIDERED THE BEST POUND-FOR-POUND MIXED MARTIAL ARTIST ON THE PLANET. HE LIVES IN CURITIBA, BRAZIL.

ERICH KRAUSS IS A PROFESSIONAL MUAY THAI KICKBOXER WHO HAS LIVED AND FOUGHT IN THAILAND. HE HAS WRITTEN FOR THE NEW YORK TIMES AND IS THE AUTHOR OF TWENTY BOOKS.

GLEN CORDOZA IS A PROFESSIONAL MUAY THAI KICKBOXER AND MIXED MARTIAL ARTS FIGHTER. HE IS THE AUTHOR OF TEN BOOKS ON THE MARTIAL ARTS.